AN ENDLESS STREAM OF LIES

A YOUNG MAN'S VOYAGE INTO FRAUD

WRITTEN BY
DON RABON

An Endless Stream of Lies

Copyright © 2015 by Don Rabon

All rights reserved. No part of this book may be reproduced or transmitted in any form or by any means without written permission of the author.

ISBN 978-0-9903367-0-9

Published by:
Highly Motivated, Inc.
Hendersonville, NC

Contents

	Preface.. i
	Introduction.. v
1	A Rip Tide of Human Actions............................. 1
2	The Search for the Source of Fraudster................. 15
3	Alex and the Fraud Triangle............................... 29 Three Atoms to Form Water – Three Requirements to Form Fraud
4	Alex Met the Investors at the Well .... 49 He Took Their Water and the Well Ran Dry
5	The River Turns and Turns Once Again .... 65 Alex Leaks to the FBI Alex's Double Knavery
6	He Looked into a Pool..................................... 89 He Fell in Love He Wasted Away
7	Oil and Water.. 111 Differing Testimonies
8	No Longer at Life's Helm.................................. 127 Into the City of Woes
9	Uncharted Waters... 137

Preface

The stage is the federal courthouse in Asheville, North Carolina. The date is February 24, 2011. The scene is a sentencing hearing before the Honorable Richard L. Vorhees, United States District Court Judge. Before Judge Vorhees stands a well-educated, highly intelligent young man (thirty-three) named Alex Klosek. Alex is slated to be sentenced for his part in the illegal diversion of over seven million dollars from over one hundred people.

In Alex's fraudulent wake are ruined lives, dreams that will never be realized and the evaporation of lifetimes of savings made possible by extraordinary personal sacrifices. People who had scrimped, saved and done without in order to be able to pass onto their children and grandchildren the opportunities for better lives, now had little or nothing left. Victims were present in the courtroom that day for Alex's sentencing. Some would speak, and others would remain silent. All were waiting for some remnant of justice as it remained for them. Many victims, those there, those choosing to stay away and those whose lives limited them to a nursing home, would be disappointed.

At his sentencing, Alex asserted:

> *I'm truly sorry for everything that has happened here, for the losses the clients have experienced, the life change, and everything that has happened. I know there have been serious negative repercussions. And it was never my intent to lose anyone's money or divert anyone's money or scheme anyone out of anything.*

Is that really the case? Does Alex indeed find himself facing a federal judge ready to impose sentencing for nothing more than a series of unintentional actions on his part? Why would Alex plead guilty if he had never intended to "lose anyone's money, divert anyone's money or scheme anyone out of anything"?

Approximately four months later on June 30, 2011, Alex reported to federal prison in Memphis, Tennessee. June 30, 2011, is significant in that it was five years ago to the day that Alex had deceptively relayed his initial account to federal authorities of his own and his partner's (Bryan Noel) fraudulent diversion.

On that last day of June, 2011, Alex walked through a life portal. With a single step he crossed a threshold. The door on that threshold would lock behind him and would not unlock for seven years. While admittedly at a country club of the federal prison system, Alex's confined life would not be his own. For seven years he will be told when to get up, go to sleep, eat and work. At the end of that seven-year period, when they return his clothing and personal belongings to him, they will hand him one more item to carry with him—a ten million dollar restitution.

An email Alex had sent to a friend was read into the transcript during Alex's cross examination. Alex was quoted as follows:

> *The idea of starting our own hedge fund sounds like a great idea. Talk about looking forward to getting up in the morning, to know that millions of dollars rests in our hands. The decisions we make could move markets. In addition, we'll have a team of people under us who do the b---s--t work, feed us the information, and then we make the decisions about where to put the money.*

How enthusiastically would Alex be "looking forward to getting up in the morning" for the next seven years? Who would be making "the decisions" in Alex's life? Who is it that would be doing "the b---s--t work"? Where was the "team of people" destined to be under Alex?

Preface

How did this all come about? A young man with no intention of doing wrong is faced with seven years' imprisonment and ten million dollars of restitution. Is this a gross miscarriage of justice? Perhaps, but not in the way you might expect. Want to find out what happened to bring this all about? Pick up a paddle, get in the boat, and let's go.

Introduction

"In mighty torrents foams the ocean
Against the rocks with roaring song—
In ever-speeding spheric motion
Both rock and sea are swept along"
—GOETHE (TRANSLATED BY WALTER KAUFMANN), FAUST

A Deal with the Devil

Fraud is inherently a matter of incentives. In Goethe's "Faust," a deal is made with the devil—Mephistopheles—who offered an incentive, a soul traded for an opportunity. A short term, temporal gain is exchanged for an eternal loss. Faust exchanges his eternal soul for the brief period of a life, yet a life lived just the way he wanted it. He opted for the prelude in lieu of the symphony.

Fraud is inherently a deal with the devil—an illegal asset transfer having inexorably high penalties for such a shift. In "Faust," the moment wherein the deal was agreed upon is easily identifiable. The devil proposed to Faust:

> *"Still, if through life you'll go with me,*
> *In that case I'll agree*
> *With pleasure to accommodate*
> *You, on the spot belong to you.*
> *I'll be your comrade true*
> *And if to your liking I behave,*
> *I'll be your servant, be your slave!"*

Faust, in seeking the additional information he needed to make his decision, asks,

> *"And what in turn am I to do for you?"*

The devil replies,

> *"Here to your service I will bind me;*
> *Beck when you will, I will not pause or rest;*
> *But in return when yonder you will find me,*
> *Then likewise shall you be at my behest."*

Once their negotiations reached agreement, the devil seals the deal with simply, *"Done!"* It was a *fait accompli*—a done deal. The devil's incentive brought about his desired goal—Faust's very soul.

But in life, it is not quite so easy to delineate the exact point wherein a person—not a literary character—makes a deal with the devil. In Reality 101, perhaps the devil does not so much appear in our private study, as in the case of Faust, but rather sits patiently at a table found within an anteroom of a human heart. He sits and waits for circumstances to draw someone into the room. The individual just happens to idly wander in as if looking for some misplaced item. He sees the devil and now must make a choice: leave the room or sit down, just to have a little talk, you see, and explore some options—check out the incentives, kick a couple of moral tires. Where's the harm in that?

An Endless Stream of Lies is not about a person that turned on their heels and immediately walked out of the room. Rather, this narrative is about someone who walked over to the table, pulled out the chair, sat down, examined the incentives, looked the devil in the eye and asked, as did Faust, "And in return, what do you want out of this?" For this person, whatever the cost, it was worth the deal—financial fraud by a modern day

Introduction

Faustian fraudster. In this exploration we will come to know both the fraud and the fraudster.

Water Under the Bridge

Finances are habitually linked to *water* related terminologies. For example, we may say or hear:

- "His resources *dried up*."
- "He had a good deal of *liquid assets*."
- "She wanted to *float a loan*."
- "The revenue *flowed* in on a regular basis."
- "The vehicle manufacturer received a *bailout*."

Parenthetically, our examination of this reality-based, Faustian character and this set of circumstances will orientate toward *water*-related terminologies. That metaphorical conceptualization is just the manner in which I process circumstances and events. I see the representational frame of a situation, in a specific circumstance, and that is how I conceptualize it from then on. Bear with me. Consequently, in our assessment, we will seek to follow this *stream* as it relates to Alex's deal with the devil, in order to find its source, adjoining *tributaries* and journey's end.

One other note I continually recommend to those whose profession necessitates investigation and interviewing: read and study classic literature. Shakespeare, Dickens, Poe and the like provide great insight into human motivations and cognitions. To me, the classics are psychology books sans the footnotes and more illustrative. Toward that end, throughout this study, we will often compare the *cascading* circumstances we encounter to relevant examples within literature. Once more, bear with me.

My goal, for this book, is broad based in the extreme. For those responsible for investigating and apprehending fraudsters, my wish is for this case study to serve as a resource, providing insight into the *flow* of precipitating events with the words, thought processes and subsequent actions of a fraudster. As a result, hopefully, it will assist in their future investigations and success in bringing other fraudsters to justice.

Additionally, for those having an interest in the human psyche, the dual nature of man, a person's actions and the consequences that follow, my hope is this will serve as opportunity to look deeply within the humanity of a specific fraud case and a unique fraudster.

As you journey along you will find:

At the top of each chapter: "**NAVIGATION POINT AND HEADING →**". This element is designed to summarize our location at this point on our journey. We are venturing into a complex set of circumstances that, at times, *flows* back upon itself. In like manner, there will be times in which we will have to trek back a bit in order to gain a more knowledgeable perspective of the situation. Knowing where we are helps a great deal in making the determination as to where we are going as we push off once again.

At the end of each chapter there will be a section titled "**THOUGHTS, COMMENTS AND ANALYSIS**." This template is designed to allow the explorer to process their assessment of the current status of the voyage, formalize their thoughts by *writing them down* and identify options for moving the inquiry forward. I encourage those wishing to maximize their experience to concentrate on this portion, in order to utilize their own abilities to conceptualize, evaluate and transition the inquiry forward.

Following that exercise, there will be a section titled "**POINTS TO PONDER**." This segment is comprised of a series of (hopefully) thought provoking questions that I provide, related to the chapter. This alternate set of questions is designed to simulate the advantages of having someone else to toss around information, thoughts, questions and action steps. Two heads really are better than one, even if one of them is mine.

Lastly, there is a "**CONTENT – CONTEXT APPLICATION**" exercise. This device is designed to provide the explorer with an opportunity to examine an additional fraud-related circumstance. The examination serves to guide the explorer towards thinking through the information provided into a more expansive application.

Introduction

Those explorers, not responsible for fraud investigations, may choose to drift on past the end-of-chapter exercises; however, anyone who appreciates a cognitive challenge may find the exercises most informative.

While providing investigative assistance to a law enforcement agency, I conducted an analysis of a homicide-related, hand written narrative that began with "Once upon a time." The homicide was related to the theft of weapons. Our current inquiry involves the theft of over seven million dollars of assets from over one hundred people. Accordingly, let us begin in likewise manner: Once upon a time . . .

CHAPTER ONE

A Rip Tide of Human Actions

The writer, like a swimmer caught by an undertow, is borne in an unexpected direction. He is carried to a subject which has awaited him—a subject sometimes no part of his conscious plan. Reality, the reality of sensation, has accumulated where it was least sought. To write is to be captured—captured by some experience to which one may have given hardly a thought.
    —Elizabeth Bowen (1899–1973), *Seven Winters*

Navigation Point and Heading → In the flow of events, our lives intersect constantly with others. In some cases, we pause and pass on as before—nothing of significance has changed. In other circumstances, however, that intersecting results in a life-course shift that can be observed and articulated. The ripple effect of a life touching a life and each in turn touching other lives, and so on, is a driving force in the course of human proceedings. Nothing happens in a vacuum. That being the case, when Alex Klosek—the central figure of our examination—and I found ourselves at an intersection, it was not a starting point for either of us, but rather, a point along a continuum. My life had unfolded along its way. His life had transitioned along its course. Now our lives were about to intersect. Ultimately, that crossing would result in a most intriguing mystery and the writing of this book.

Note: Fraud Defined: *"Intentional perversion of truth in order to induce another to part with something of value or to surrender a legal right"* (www.merriam-webster.com).

The Intersection of Two Lives

To put it directly, I have spent over thirty years working my way into and around the minds of people who deviated from the norms of society. I have investigated and interviewed murderers, kidnappers, pedophiles, fraudsters and most crimes in between. People, what they do and why they do it, have been and continue to be a continual source of intriguing study for me.

Having the ability to develop a rapport with people whose behaviors flow against the tide of acceptable behavior, and learning how "things" operate in their world, has allowed me to pass along insights, skills and understanding to thousands of investigative and other related personnel who must deal with aberrant behavior on a daily basis as a function of their profession.

The journey has carried me around the world providing interview and investigative training and assistance to a variety of organizations and individuals. I have published other books, all directed toward questioning, detecting deception, persuading, and understanding another's cognition. That portion is the work side of my life, and it is a source of never-ending interest and challenge.

In my separate, though equally satisfying, personal life, the interviewing, investigative and discourse analysis related skills lie dormant. I enjoy my family and friends, never thinking of parsing their words, looking for subtle changes in behavior or evaluating their veracity. I like people, and I want them to feel comfortable being with me. My 2004 Road King Custom Harley Davidson motorcycle, scuba diving, classical literature, and writing provide ample opportunities to meet and interact with others all the while just being me.

But in 2006, a passageway connecting the two distinct dimensions of my life suddenly opened. Alex Klosek, an acquaintance and member of the Sunday Bible study class I teach, asked me to meet him at Kelsey's

Restaurant in Hendersonville, North Carolina, for lunch. At the time I was serving as Deputy Director for the Larry T. Justus Western Campus of the North Carolina Justice Academy, a division of the North Carolina Department of Justice, and was a year away from my thirty-year retirement. For twenty years prior to my promotion to Deputy Director, I had been privileged to be the manager of the Investigations Center for the Academy. That was the best job I ever had.

In the course of our lunch, Alex informed me he had recently met with representatives of the Federal Bureau of Investigation with an admission to his own, as well as his business partner, Bryan Noel's, fraudulent activities. This fraud had taken place over a number of years through their operations—Certified Estate Planners, a local investment firm—as well as a multitude of other companies and financial entities they had formed as vehicles to divert monies.

Immediately, my "focus on behavior" antenna began to go up. Concurrently, the interviewer–investigator dial in my head started toward the "on" position like a compass arrow moving toward magnetic north. In the opening moments of a professional communication event, commonly referred to as an "interview," I, like most interviewers, transition into "the zone." At this point, the attention given to the interviewee's verbal, vocal and nonverbal behaviors goes to the highest level. His words and mannerisms are evaluated in context. Each response is framed and leads to the next elicitation option. An interview-based outcome is identified or modified accordingly, and all of the interviewer's stimuli are directed toward that goal. Once underway, it is like a large, ocean-going exploratory vessel—very difficult to stop on a dime.

"Wait a minute." I reflected, "This is not your case. This is a member of the Sunday Bible study and he is talking to you as such." Consequently, through no small effort on my part, the antenna retracted most of the way, the investigator dial was reset close to the "off" position, and my mental engine order telegraph was set at "slow ahead." I would be less than honest if I intimated that all capabilities had been shut down. Even in the

3

conversational mode, my investigator knowledge that there is no coincidence in life caused me to reflect. I wondered, "Was Alex in my Sunday Bible study because of who I was and the position I occupied with the North Carolina Department of Justice?" Later, when he asked for a letter of reference for the judge to consider during the sentencing phase (which I did not submit), the dots were connected—at least in my mind.

What he had to say then and other times we met over the course of five years, on an irregular basis, varied from personal issues to particulars about the case and the ongoing investigation. He did not ask for advice, and I offered none. When we met, I purposely avoided asking investigative-related questions. I did not need to. After the phatic phase of our communication transpired, off he went without any prompting on my part. I listened and responded as his Bible study teacher. I did note, however, that at no time in all of our meetings did Alex express remorse for the grief and loss he and his business partner had inflicted upon so many people. The conversation always flowed to him and the prevailing circumstances, acting upon him, as he perceived it.

Shortly after the initial meeting, the details of the case became public and served as the area media's item of choice with each new revelation, accusation or new stage of the proceedings. Hendersonville is a small, mountain community in western North Carolina with a disproportional amount of wealthy retirees—local and transplanted. While the diverted funds' range of seven to ten million dollars might not seem like a great deal of money in comparison to the billions Bernie Madoff had stolen, in Hendersonville, each meeting of the irate investors was good for front page, above-the-fold material, as well as the area's electronic media's "this just in" moments for those reading from the teleprompters.

Alex had seemingly revealed to the federal investigators the fraudulent activities that he and his co-conspirator had undertaken over the course of several years. Their scheming drained the resources from over one hundred people. Additionally, the harm to the government as a result of their activities in this case was valued at fifty-five million dollars. Alex appeared to assist the federal authorities by wearing a body mike during conversations with Noel in addition to recording some of their subsequent phone conversations.

For his cooperative efforts, Alex was given a deal. He would be allowed to plead to one count with a maximum sentence of five years and a fine of up to $250,000. The federal government's press release regarding Alex's plea agreement read as follows:

"DEPARTMENT OF JUSTICE

*Acting United States Attorney Edward R. Ryan
Western District of North Carolina*

FOR IMMEDIATE RELEASE
FRIDAY, JUNE 12, 2009

CONTACT: Terry Wilkinson
704.344.6222
Fax: 704.344.0629

ETOWAH, NORTH CAROLINA MAN SIGNS PLEA AGREEMENT IN FEDERAL CRIMINAL CASE INVOLVING CERTIFIED ESTATE PLANNERS, INC. ASHEVILLE, NC. —*Alexander Klosek, 31, of Etowah, North Carolina, was charged today in a federal bill of information filed in U.S. District Court in Asheville, with one count alleging conspiracy to commit mail and wire fraud. Klosek has agreed to plead guilty to the charge pursuant to a plea agreement with the government, also filed today. Dates have not yet been set for the formal entry of Klosek's guilty plea or for Klosek's sentencing.*

Acting U.S. Attorney Edward R. Ryan is joined by Owen Harris, Special Agent in Charge of the FBI in North Carolina, in making today's announcement. The charge against Klosek arises out of an alleged conspiracy in which he participated and which took place from in or about January 2003 through about June 2006 in Henderson County, involving Certified Estate Planners, Inc. The bill of information filed against Alexander Klosek alleges that he, together with B.N. and others, solicited over 100 investors to invest large sums of their retirement savings with Certified Estate Planners, Inc. ("CEP") by promising a conservative investment strategy. Today's charging bill of information also states that Klosek and B.N., without CEP clients' knowledge, diverted several million dollars of the clients' assets to B.N.'s start-up lumber composite company, thereby significantly decreasing the value of the clients' investments. The bill of information states that Klosek and B.N. then continually misrepresented the *value of the clients' assets on the quarterly statements mailed to clients so that they would not know the true diminished value of their assets. Based on this scheme, the CEP clients were defrauded of approximately $7 million.*

The Federal Bureau of Investigation led the investigation that resulted in the filing of today's bill of information and in the filing of a related bill of indictment, filed June 3, 2009, alleging that Bryan Noel also participated in the above-described conspiracy. The government has also been assisted in this investigation by the North Carolina Secretary of State's Office.

The government is represented in this matter by Assistant U.S. Attorney Melissa Rikard of the U.S. Attorney's Criminal Division in Charlotte. Also today in federal court in Asheville, Bryan Noel was afforded a detention hearing before U.S. Magistrate Judge Dennis L. Howell. Noel was ordered detained.

A copy of the bill of information charging Alexander Klosek is provided along with this press release. Klosek faces a maximum penalty of five years' imprisonment, a $250,000 fine, or both.

ALEXANDER KLOSEK
Age: 31
Etowah, North Carolina"

Noel had been arrested, placed in jail with no opportunity for bail and scheduled for trial. The federal government's press release regarding his charges and arrest read as follows:

"Department of Justice Press Release
United States Attorney's Office
Western District of North Carolina
Contact: (704) 344-6222

For Immediate Release
June 4, 2009

Bryan Noel Indicted for Conspiracy and Mail Fraud
Former Owner of CEP, Inc. Charged in 28-Count Federal Indictment

ASHEVILLE, NC—Bryan Noel, 39, of Hendersonville, NC, has been indicted and arrested on one count alleging conspiracy to commit mail fraud, 25 separate counts alleging mail fraud, and two separate counts alleging making a false oath in connection with a bankruptcy proceeding, all in connection with an investment scheme which resulted in losses of approximately $7 million. Noel made his initial appearance before a U.S. Magistrate Judge today and was detained pending a hearing. That hearing is scheduled for Friday, June 5, 2009, at 12:00 p.m.

Today's announcement is made by Edward R. Ryan, Acting United States Attorney for the Western District of North Carolina, and Owen Harris, Special Agent in Charge of the Federal Bureau of Investigation (FBI) in North Carolina.

"We know that numerous victims have waited a long time for this day," said Acting U.S. Attorney Ryan. "We believe that the filing of these allegations is the first of many steps toward seeing justice served and recouping some of their losses," he added.

According to the indictment, which was returned by a federal grand jury sitting in Asheville on June 3 and filed under seal, from around January 2003 until about July 2006, in Henderson County, Noel and others solicited over 100 clients to invest large sums of their retirement savings with Certified Estate Planners, Inc. ("CEP") by promising a conservative investment strategy. The indictment alleges that in about 1999 Noel created CEP to solicit investors and to offer estate planning services geared toward retirees. The indictment alleges that shortly after the initial investments were collected, without the investors' knowledge, several million dollars of the investors' assets were diverted, thereby significantly decreasing the value of the investments. According to the allegations contained in the indictment, those funds were diverted to Noel's start-up lumber composite company. The indictment alleges that thereafter the value of the assets was continually misrepresented on the quarterly statements mailed to investors so that they would not know the true diminished value of their assets. In summary, the indictment alleges that by July 2006, Noel and an unindicted co-conspirator had misrepresented to investors that their assets had grown to a total of approximately $16 million, when in reality, investors' assets had shrunk to only approximately $1 million. According to the indictment, Noel filed for Chapter 7 bankruptcy protection in August of 2007.

Noel is separately charged in counts two through twenty-six with substantive violations of mail fraud alleging that he used the U.S. mail to cause false quarterly statements to be delivered to his investors for the purpose of further executing his alleged scheme to defraud. The indictment was unsealed following the arrest of Bryan Noel earlier today.

If convicted, Noel faces a maximum sentence of 20 years' imprisonment on each of the conspiracy and mail fraud counts, five years' imprisonment on each of the counts alleging false oaths in a bankruptcy proceeding, and a maximum $250,000 fine for each count.

The case was investigated by the FBI, and the prosecution is being handled by Assistant U.S. Attorney Melissa Rikard of the Western District of North Carolina.

An Endless Stream of Lies

The details contained in the indictment are allegations. The defendant is presumed innocent unless and until proven guilty beyond a reasonable doubt in a court of law."

In the functioning of a fraud-related case of this nature, that pattern is the gold standard. Noel would be tried, Alex would testify for the prosecution regarding his and Noel's criminal activities, and a verdict would be rendered. Following the trial disposition, Alex would be sentenced and, judicially, that would have been that. As it happened, Bryan Noel was tried and found guilty of twenty-three of twenty-four federal charges in March of 2010. The charges included "mail fraud, money laundering, conspiracy and bankruptcy fraud." The jury took only six-and-a-half hours of deliberation after a two week trial to reach a verdict.

But for the federal authorities, this case was to prove to be anything but standard, and most assuredly not golden. Shortly before Bryan Noel's trial was scheduled to begin, revelations with regard to Alex's five-year continued deception of them and asset diversions after his apparent willingness to cooperate, came to the surface.

On Super Bowl Sunday of 2010, Alex asked if I would stop by his house after lunch. While at his house, Alex disclosed to me that he had deceived the federal agents and prosecutors from the beginning of his 2006 meetings and cooperative efforts with them, all while holding onto diverted assets. Noel's defense team had discovered his continued deception and diversion, and they had made the federal prosecutors aware. As a result of his continued manipulations, his previous deal was taken off of the table and he now faced up to twenty years.

At his house that afternoon, I said to him, "Alex, in all of our meetings over these years you have never asked me for advice. I am telling you now, nevertheless, that you had better cooperate with the federal agents and prosecutors to the fullest." I made no effort to try and obtain a commitment on his part to do so, left, returned home and watched the game.

In the fullness of time, it became known publicly that Alex had indeed deceived the federal authorities from the beginning of his meetings with them and had subsequently kept possession of diverted resources. Far and away, his actions had certainly deviated from the "standard" of a fraud case of this category.

Now that an access between my professional life and personal life had been reopened by Alex's most recent revelations, there was no closing it. I had to know. Of all the people I have known, interviewed, studied or investigated, Alex is one of the most enigmatic. He is highly intellectual, articulate and has a dry—one really has to look for it—sense of humor. But it was the duality of Alex's life—the daylight "see you in church" side co-existing with the dark "continuing to deceive and steal" side—that compelled me to stay the course.

THE DUALITY OF MAN

The duality of man is not in and of itself an uncommon occurrence. There is the good and bad in all of us. Even the Apostle Paul struggled with the conflict between his mindset and his actions—"For that which I do *I allow not: for what I would, that do I not; but what I hate, that do I*" (Romans 7:15). But with Alex, the circumstances were dramatically different. For Alex, to continue to deceive and steal after he had obtained (in light of the circumstance) a generous offer from the federal prosecutor, set him far apart from the run-of-the-mill fraudster. Here was an individual who deceived his client-investors, his partner, and continued paddling deceptively up to and right past the federal authorities. A "morbidity deceiver" is one who continues to deceive when it would be in their best interest to tell the truth. But in light of the fraud-incentive, Faustian dynamic, the question is, "In their best interest as defined by whom?"

As Alex moved into deeper water, his story unfolds in a manner not unlike a Shakespearian tragedy. Classically, we wonder, who was the "real" Hamlet? Personally, I wondered, who was the real Alex? Was Alex just a bit of flotsam pulled out to a sea of fraud by a riptide over which he had no control? Or was Alex so diabolical that he had planned and carried out a deception, within a deception, within a deception? Why was his "deal with the devil" more attractive to him than his deal with the prosecutor? What incentive did the continued deception offer that was greater than that offered by the prosecutor?

A riptide is "a strong channel of water flowing seaward from near the shore, typically through the surf line." It occurs "when wind and waves push water towards the shore, that water is often forced sideways by the oncoming waves. This water streams along the shoreline until it finds an exit back to the sea or open lake water" (Wikipedia.com). The Greek word for riptide is *anaklusmos*. Its literal meaning is "to wash against (*ana* = against, *klyzein* = wash)" (Reference.com). Were there external "winds and waves" that ultimately carried Alex out on a riptide of deception? On the other hand, Alex had indeed "washed against" a variety of people sweeping their resources out to sea. Was Alex, in reality, not so much the floating debris, but rather the riptide itself?

In this theater of life drama, we find conflict between father and son and between co-conspirators. We discover deception of investors as well as federal authorities, betrayal, intrigue and more.

An Endless Stream of Lies is my search for an understanding of Alex and his actions. This is not a search to provide an opportunity to be critical of Alex. We will allow Alex's own actions and words, as he responds to questions in open court, to define him. We will utilize segments from the transcripts from Noel's trial and Alex's sentencing hearing as navigational devices. I have placed the emphasis on the questions that were asked of Alex and his subsequent revelations. Who asked the questions of Alex is secondary. Alex's answers are primary. As you move forward, examine carefully Alex's answers to the questions that were asked. When a person tells us about "things," they in turn tell us about themselves. Keep his answers in context to his answers to previous questions as well as his actions.

This examination of his story is a journey to know a fraudster by his actions, his words, the subsequent downstream consequences of his undertakings and the insights I can uncover and pass along to other fraud-related investigative personnel.

A Rip Tide of Human Actions

In his writings, Shakespeare drew from history, legends, characters from life, and the circumstances in which they were moved or drawn. In this unfolding of Alex's voyage into the abyss, if Shakespeare were alive today he would most certainly be saying, "And then what happened?" If my grandmother, Lacy Watts Brown, who spent her life from ages nine to sixty-five standing on her feet, working in a cotton mill in Belmont, North Carolina, were alive today, she would answer him, "It'll all come out in the wash."

Thoughts, Comments and Analysis

What are your impressions, to this point, with regard to this circumstance?

Exactly what do you know?

What is it that you **know** that you don't know?

What questions would you ask in order to know?

What steps would you take in order to know?

A Rip Tide of Human Actions

Points to Ponder

01. Why would Alex want to meet with me specifically from the time of his initial meeting with federal authorities until the revelation of his continued deception?

02. Why would Alex continue to deceive and divert resources after having made a deal with the federal prosecutor?

03. Why would Alex, a highly intelligent, educated individual, involve himself in a situation that he knew could potentially have profound, adverse consequences to his life?

04. What questions could have been asked of Alex on the day he first met with federal authorities?

05. At what point would someone come to trust an individual who is an admitted fraudster?

06. What questions would you pose to Alex at this point?

Content – Context Application

Ex-fireman Charged

An ex-fireman faced seventy-one counts for embezzling $226,000 from a firefighters association and a volunteer fire department. He also was charged with five counts of obtaining money by false pretense. He had previously served as the president of the association and as the assistant chief of the fire department. Additionally, through his activities at his place of employment, he was charged with taking $45,000 from three clients with the promise to invest the money into an annuity. The clients notified the company when they never received any paperwork related to their annuity purchases.

01. What might be the commonalities of circumstances that we have reviewed in Alex's circumstance and the ex-fireman?

02. What might be the differences of circumstances between the two?

03. How does the dynamic of trust others (clients, partner, federal authorities) placed in Alex factor into the entire circumstance?

04. How does the dynamic of trust others (fire department and place of employment) placed in the ex-fireman factor into the entire circumstance?

05. What questions would you pose to this individual?

CHAPTER TWO

The Search for the Source of Fraudster

> Time is a sort of river of passing events, and strong is its current; no sooner is a thing brought to sight than it is swept by and another takes its place, and this too will be swept away.
> —Marcus Aurelius

Navigation Point and Heading → Nothing happens in a vacuum. There is no coincidence in life. Events, like rivers, have a beginning—a starting point from which there is an increasing flow toward the middle and onward to a precise finality. Identifying the end of the river or the event is not especially difficult. It is discovering the beginning that proves to be most challenging. Where exactly does the river begin? Likewise, at what precise point did Alex launch on his voyage into the abyss? More importantly perhaps is "Why?"

Where Did It Begin – Where is the Source?

The beginning of a river is known as the "source." In the 1800s, there was a great undertaking to find the source of the Nile. A prize was offered for the explorer who made the discovery. Some of the famous explorers participating in the quest were Richard Burton, John Hanning Speke, Sir Samuel White Baker, Henry Morton Stanley, James Augustus Grant and

Dr. David Livingstone. For their times, the task was much more daunting than what we might think of today with satellite technology allowing for a look at the world from an all-encompassing perspective. There was, and continues to be today, a complex, geographical set of circumstances that made the search to find the beginning of the Nile no easy undertaking. With regard to Alex, our search for the headwaters as the source of his fraudulent machinations is a similar challenge. In order to work our way back up river to the source, we have to begin with the first step.

It is a Long Way Back

In the beginning of our exploration, we will utilize as our map the **"Complaint For Permanent Injunction And For Other Relief** Case 1:07-cv-00306, filed September 24, 2007," in The United States District Court for the Western District of North Carolina. The complaint was filed by the United States Department of Justice. As you read through the complaint, you will gain an appreciation for the complexity of investigating and prosecuting crimes of this nature. Concurrently, gain and maintain an appreciation for those responsible for the investigation and prosecution thereof.

As we progress through this and the subsequent chapters, we will incorporate other sources, including Alex's own testimony, to gain understanding.

Step by step, throughout the text we will endeavor to trace back through Alex's course of activities, to examine what transpired. Along our way, we will discover specific junctions—individuals coming together, forming companies, advertising, meeting with perspective clients, gaining their trust, taking their money and using it for their own purposes. Each of these junctions serves as an additional branch flowing into the larger stream of Alex's life. Like any explorer, our collective goal is to "know" and ultimately, "understand." *Knowing* tells us *what*. *Understanding* tells us *why*. In this case also, we want to know "when" and "how" the seemingly still waters of Alex's life took on a destructive undercurrent that did, in fact, run treacherous and deep.

The complaint discloses:

Alex had been preparing tax returns since 1999 (49). He was "neither a licensed nor registered tax return preparer" but rather what is termed "an unenrolled tax return preparer" (12).

In 1999, Alex's co-conspirator, Brian Noel, incorporated Certified Estate Planners, Inc. The company was designed to allow him to sell trusts. Brian was the president of Certified Estate Planners, Inc. (7).

NOTE: *"What Does Trust Mean?*

> *A fiduciary relationship in which one party, known as a trustor, gives another party, the trustee, the right to hold title to property or assets for the benefit of a third party, the beneficiary. The assets held in the trust can include, but are not limited to, a business, investment assets, cash and life insurance policies" (www.investopedia.com)*

In September, 1999, Noel founded Pinnacle Advisors, LLC. "Pinnacle Advisors was set up as a trustee company to provide trustee services (i.e., managing assets, securities, annuities, insurance contracts, etc.) for the irrevocable trusts of Certified Estate Planners, Inc.'s customers" (14).

NOTE: *"What Does Irrevocable Trust Mean?*

> *A trust that can't be modified or terminated without the permission of the beneficiary. The grantor, having transferred assets into the trust, effectively removes all of his or her rights of ownership to the assets and the trust.*
>
> *The main reason for setting up an irrevocable trust is for estate and tax considerations. The benefit of this type of trust for estate assets is that it removes all incidents of ownership, effectively removing the trust's assets from the grantor's taxable estate. The grantor is also relieved of the tax liability on the income generated by the assets. While the tax rules will vary between jurisdictions, in most*

cases, the grantor can't receive these benefits if he or she is the trustee of the trust." (www.investopedia.com)

Alex "began working with Noel in May, 2000" (11). The merging of these two streams—Alex and Noel—marks a significant connection. Pause here a moment, look around and contemplate. Without Alex, the possibility of the fraudulent activity involving the same victims occurring still existed. But, what could have been the course of events in Alex's life had he not met Noel and subsequently began to work with him? How differently would the current of his life have flowed had these two streams never intersected? Would it have flowed differently but reached the same destination?

Two Drops of Water

That day in May, 2000, when Alex began working with Noel was not the source of the fraud but rather a contributing factor, making it possible to happen. In Henderson County, North Carolina, Highway 64 East runs from Hendersonville to Bat Cave. Along the way, it passes through the picturesque, apple-farming community of Edneyville.

There, by the roadside, the traveler will find a sign indicating the point of the eastern continental divide. To the east of the sign, rain water will flow to the Atlantic Ocean. West of the sign, rain water will find its way to the Gulf of Mexico. Whether the rain falls to the east or the west of the divide is determined by a set of variables over which the drops have no control. These variables include but are not limited to wind, humidity, gravity, temperature, cloud type and barometric pressure. It is possible for two raindrops to begin their fall from the cloud to earth side by side; however, due to the actions of the variables, one drop falls east of the divide and the other falls to the west. While on the journeys to their respective destinations, one drop could serve as part of a lifesaving drink of water, while the other drop could be part of the water that fills the lungs of a drowning victim.

That day in May, 2000, Alex was the drop of water leaving the cloud. What were the factors which would ultimately place him on the deceptive side of the divide? How did he come to land on the wrong side of the divide between right and wrong that carried him downward to fraud, deception and ultimately—to the abyss?

In Shakespeare's *Hamlet*, scene III, act III, the concept of small events resulting in dire consequences is presented when Rosencrantz speaks:

> *"To whose huge spokes ten thousand lesser things*
> *Are mortised and adjoin'd; which, when it falls,*
> *Each small annexment, petty consequence,*
> *Attends the boisterous ruin. Never alone*
> *Did the King sigh, but with a general groan."*

When Alex met Noel and subsequently began working with him, it was—in the daily course of human interactions—a seemingly "lesser thing." Such connections happen multiple times on a daily basis. It is possible that on a number of levels—personally, socially and economically—those who were previously strangers can form a relationship, go forth and, through their financial undertakings, legitimately benefit themselves and others. For example, somewhere along the line Ben met Jerry, and many of us enjoy their ice cream. Mr. Harley joined Mr. Davidson, and it made for the world's best motorcycle.

But when Alex met Noel, a prosperous and legitimate outcome was not to be the case. From this meeting, the downstream consequences were indeed "boisterous ruin." At the point when they met for the first time, the over one hundred people destined to be washed over by the "annexment" of one small stream uniting with another did not cry out with a "general groan." Their lamentations would only be heard years later. And while they were affected collectively, they individually felt the pain personally. Like a tsunami pouring over hundreds of people at once, they all would be drowned individually. Ultimately, Alex, in his own manner, would be drowned also.

On the day Alex and Noel met, none of the destined-to-be victims of their fraud felt as if someone had walked over their grave. Were it the case that they all futilely consulted a horoscope that day, they would have found no financial caution in the stars applying to a multitude of different birthdays. No, it was but one of a multitude of "lesser things" that, in the aggregate, proved to be disastrous. The companies were formed and the positions were appointed—all lesser tributaries leading to tribulation. These tributaries had names such as Certified Estate Planners, Silverado Financial Group, Pinnacle Fiduciary and Trust, International Titanium Corporation, and International Mineral Exchange.

"In 2000, Noel was the subject of an IRS audit. During this audit, the revenue agent informed Noel that the trust he was using personally was not valid and the agent made substantial adjustments to his income taxes. During the audit, Noel stated that he now understood that the trust was invalid for income tax purposes. After the audit, Noel continued to market and create substantially similar 'trusts' for his customers" (45).

"Alex and Noel founded the company Silverado Financial Group, Inc. in February 2001. The purpose of the company was to facilitate the preparation of returns for the trust customers. They founded Silverado as equal partners. Alex was listed as the registered agent for Silverado (11). Alex conducted business as Silverado while he prepared tax returns for the trust customers" (17).

"In March 2001, Noel and Alex formed Pinnacle Fiduciary and Trust as an 'irrevocable' trust for the purpose of managing all of the clients' assets. Alex served as the trustee for Pinnacle Fiduciary and Trust" (15).

"On September 5, 2001, Alex became the registered agent of Certified Estate Planners, Inc. (11). On that same day Alex became the registered agent for Pinnacle Advisors and began performing trustee services and preparing income-tax returns for customers" (14).

"Alex's activities included preparing customers' trust returns and managing customer's investments by transferring the funds to various accounts and conducting short-term stock trades. Alex was neither a licensed nor a registered tax return preparer" (12).

"Alex was operating as an unlicensed broker and was not registered with the Securities Exchange Commission to sell securities. Neither was Alex a Certified Financial Planner" (13).

"In 2002 the IRS began audits of Alex and Noel's customers who had purchased "irrevocable living trusts" (28). "After this investigation commenced, they ceased selling the 'irrevocable living trusts.' That same year they began selling 'revocable asset management trusts'" (29). "Alex and Noel had marketed the revocable asset management trusts to their customers as a way to avoid taxes on their investments" (30).

NOTE: *"What Does Revocable Trust Mean?*

> *"A trust whereby provisions can be altered or canceled dependent on the grantor. During the life of the trust, income earned is distributed to the grantor, and only after death does property transfer to the beneficiaries. Also referred to as a "revocable living trust". This type of agreement provides flexibility and income to the living grantor; he or she is able to adjust the provisions of the trust and earn income, all the while knowing that the estate will be transferred upon death." (www.investopedia.com)*

"In 2002, Noel received a letter from an investor's attorney detailing the invalidity of the trust and threatening suit against Noel and Certified Estate Planners, Inc. Specifically, the letter detailed that the customers were not properly advised about the consequences of the transfer of assets to the trust, nor was the trust an appropriate estate planning, income tax, or asset protection strategy. Noel showed the letter to an attorney" (46).

"After receiving and reading the letter Noel had shown to him, the attorney warned Noel about the trusts he was promoting. The letter caused the attorney to question the validity of the trusts. As a result, the attorney conducted his own research on the validity of the trusts and was unable to find any legal or tax information to support these types of trusts. The attorney informed Noel of that finding in writing" (47).

"From 2000 to 2002 Alex and Noel sold 'irrevocable trust' tax schemes" (18). "The sole purpose of these 'trusts' was to evade the customer's tax obligations" (19). "In marketing the 'trusts,' Noel would target primarily wealthy elderly customers to join Certified Estate Planners, Inc. Advertisement was made through flyers, conferences, and via their website" (20).

"These advertisements falsely claimed that the customers would be able to avoid their income taxes by placing their assets in trust while still continuing to 'manag[e] everything' but 'own nothing'" (21). "Once a customer joined, Alex and Noel would create an individual 'irrevocable trust' for that customer. Each trust would obtain an Employer Identification Number (EIN) from the IRS. These 'trusts' typically listed Alex as a trustee and Noel as co-trustee" (22).

"After the trust was established, customers would withdraw assets from their retirement accounts, IRAs, annuities and other deferred tax devices and deposit the funds into their 'irrevocable trust.' The customers then used these assets for personal expenses such as mortgage payments and home repairs" (23).

"The early withdrawal of these funds and subsequent use for non-tax-exempt purposes should have resulted in the assets being subject to taxation and early withdrawal penalties. As a result, the income should have been reported on the customer's individual federal income tax return. However, Alex and Noel's scheme resulted in the customer not reporting this taxable income" (24).

"As part of this scheme, Alex prepared customers' Form 1040 Individual Federal Tax Return and Form 1041 Federal Tax returns for the customer's 'trust.' Instead of reporting the withdrawn assets as personal income subject to taxation on the customer's individual Form 1040, Alex improperly reported the customer's withdrawn funds on the customer's Form 1041 'trust' tax return. Further, Alex would consistently under-report the total amount of this income on the Form" (25).

"After reporting this taxable income on the wrong form, Alex would make fraudulent deductions on the customer's Form 1041 return to fully deduct, or 'zero out,' the income reported. This would result in customers paying nominal, if any, taxes on this income. Alex improperly listed personal expenses (such as mortgage payments, utility bills, rent, and health insurance) as deductions on the customer's Form 1041 trust return" (26). "Alex would further reduce the customer's reported income by reporting large K-1 distribution fees, claiming that the customer's 'trust' distributed the income to the customer. However, these large 'distributions' were not then reported on the customer's Form 1040" (27).

"As part of this scheme Alex and Noel created a new trust, Pinnacle Fiduciary and Trust Group (PFTG), designating Alex as the trustee. As before, the customers transferred all their assets into the PFTG trust. This 'trust' was designed to be a meta-trust, meaning it held all of the assets of all of PFTG's customers in one trust. They commingled the customers' funds in order to conceal them from the IRS" (31).

"Once deposited into this 'trust' they did not track the individual customers' funds. As a result all of the various customers' funds became indistinguishable and they were unable to determine the value of each customer's 'investment'" (32). "They would then use the funds in the PFTG 'trust' to 'invest' at their discretion" (33). "These 'investments' consisted of Alex and Noel making short-term trades, 'investing' money in Noel's enjoined mineral business, and withdrawing large account management fees" (34).

"Customers were not aware of their 'investments' and they only issued reports of the customer's account activity upon request. However, these reports did not accurately represent the customer's account 'activity' because they were unable to determine which percentage of the PFTG 'trust' belonged to an individual customer" (35).

"They used the PFTG 'trust' as a shelter to hide their customers' assets from the IRS and avoid their correct income tax responsibility" (36). "They evaded taxes by falsely reporting trust performance on a Form 1041, utilizing arbitrary amounts that eliminated the tax liabilities. In essence, these returns underreported the customers' tax liabilities by not accurately reporting the basis for tax calculations, such as income earned on the customer's assets in the meta-trust, early withdrawal penalties, and capital gains the customer would have incurred" (37). "As a result, the customers evaded taxation of income earned on assets held in the PFTG trust by claiming that the assets were fully distributed" (38).

"Additionally, they did not issue Forms 1099 (forms that report non-wage income) to all of their customers; instead, they only issued the Forms 1099 to those customers who requested the information. However, even on the Forms 1099 that they did issue, they were unable to report the accurate gains and losses for each customer because they had combined all customers' assets and failed to keep records. As a result they reported arbitrary amounts" (39).

And so the stream of lies began and continued to flow (as shown by the information presentation of *Complaint For Permanent Injunction And For Other Relief* in the preceding paragraphs) with increasingly disastrous potential. But the question is, "Began at what point?" From having read the complaint above, we can only see the surface of the water. The real dangers lie in wait below the surface. For years, to the investors, and even to Alex's partner, the waters looked fine. The surface was calm and there were no warning signs posted along the banks.

In Shakespeare's *King Henry VI*, part II, act III, scene I, we learn, "by wicked means to frame our sovereign's fall. Smooth runs the water where the brook is deep." The brook was indeed deep, and sovereigns, whether considered as money or people, did, with a certainty, fall. Alex's undertakings to frame, and thus control, that fall were there, hidden just below the surface.

As we plunge below the surface to plumb the depths, we are mindful that fraud is a human construct. Humans—in this case Alex—are motivated toward gain and more emphatically away from pain. Alex has, at this point, already undertaken drastic steps for the first dynamic—gain—and will in time take action regarding the latter—the avoidance of pain.

Thoughts, Comments and Analysis

What are your impressions, to this point, with regard to this circumstance?

Exactly what do you know?

What is it that you **know** that you don't know?

What questions would you ask in order to know?

What steps would you take in order to know?

Points to Ponder

In contrasting the elements in the "Complaint For Permanent Injunction And For Other Relief Case 1:07-cv-00306, filed September 24, 2007" with Alex's words at his sentencing:

> *And it was never my intent to lose anyone's money or divert anyone's money or scheme anyone out of anything.*

01. What are your initial impressions from the comparison?

02. Is it conceivable that someone could machinate these complexities while having no intent to lose, divert or scheme?

03. What could possibly be Alex's plan once the injunction was published, yet all the while, he was continuing to deceive the federal authorities?

04. Why would he view his continued deception as his best option?

05. If actions do speak louder than words, to which of the two is it most advantageous to attend?

06. What questions would you pose to Alex at this point?

CONTENT – CONTEXT APPLICATION

Former Controller of Luxury Car Dealership Accused of Embezzling

A former controller of a luxury car dealership was charged in a federal indictment for embezzling approximately $285,000. The charges involved making and possessing forged securities with the intent to deceive. The indictment indicated the former controller had issued over 130 company commercial checks to a variety of entities and individuals. He then would deposit the checks into bank accounts that were controlled by him. He was accused of forging the endorsements on the back of the checks in order to make the deposits.

01. What similar mindsets might there be as demonstrated by the actions of Alex and the controller?

02. Is there, in your mind, a difference in defrauding an organization as opposed to defrauding an individual?

03. Why or why not?

04. What questions would you pose to this individual?

CHAPTER THREE

Alex and the Fraud Triangle
Three Atoms to Form Water – Three Requirements to Form Fraud

Water, water, every where,
And all the boards did shrink;
Water, water, every where,
Nor any drop to drink.
The Rime of the Ancient Mariner
　　—Samuel Taylor Coleridge

Navigation Point and Heading → The chemical formula for water is H_2O. A molecule of water is comprised of two hydrogen atoms and one oxygen atom. The atoms are connected by a type of chemical bonding that involves the sharing of pairs of electrons (Wikipedia.org). Fraud is also comprised of three components. These components must, in like fashion, be bonded or connected. In the case of fraud, the connections involve the circumstances in a person's life, the latitude in which they have to operate and their adaptive cognitions. How does an individual's (in this case, Alex) life-changing circumstances come down to a diagram? Paddle on and let's see.

The Fraud Triangle

In the 1950s, criminologist Donald R. Cressey presented what has classically become known as "the fraud triangle." He theorized that for the commission of fraud to take place, three components must be in place:

- Pressure/motive
- Opportunity
- Rationalization

His proposal has stood the test of time and is very much a part of fraud investigative applications today. Various entities have applied the terminology over time to a multitude of circumstances. One of the most salient, fraud-related issues, at the time of this writing, involves teachers and educational administrators manipulating the end of grade test scores by providing the answers to the students in advance or changing the students' incorrect answers after the fact. But, the concept is still the same. Once an incentive (economic, moral or societal) is attached to an outcome, two of the three fraud-related elements are subsequently in play. In the teacher–administrator case, the incentive is economic.

At this point, we have an overview of the topography of this financial water system. Let's endeavor to find the source of a specific tributary—Alex's debilitating stock trading activities and subsequent false financial reports. This undertaking involves a four-year tributary that systematically evaporated resources that belonged to others.

Statement on Auditing Standards No. 99: Consideration of Fraud in a Financial Statement Audit

First, an explanation of the "Statement on Auditing Standards No. 99: Consideration of Fraud in a Financial Statement Audit" will assist in our understanding of the relationship of the fraud triangle, the actions which Alex had undertaken and their downstream consequences:

NOTE: **What is SAS 99?**

*"**Statement on Auditing Standards No. 99: Consideration of Fraud in a Financial Statement Audit**, commonly abbreviated as **SAS 99**, is an auditing statement issued by the Auditing Standards Board of the American Institute of Certified Public Accountants (AICPA) in October 2002. The original exposure draft was distributed in February 2002. SAS 99, which supersedes SAS 82, was issued partly in response to recent accounting scandals at Enron, WorldCom, Adelphia, and Tyco. The standard incorporates recommendations from various contributors including the International Auditing & Assurance Standards Board. SAS 99 became effective for audits of financial statements for periods beginning on or after December 15, 2002" (Wikipedia.org).*

NOTE: **How does SAS 99 describe fraud?**

"SAS 99 defines fraud as an intentional act that results in a material misstatement in financial statements. There are two types of fraud considered: misstatements arising from fraudulent financial reporting (eg. falsification of accounting records) and misstatements arising from misappropriation of assets (eg. theft of assets or fraudulent expenditures").

NOTE: **How does SAS describe the fraud triangle?**

*"The standard describes the fraud triangle. Generally, the three '**fraud triangle**' conditions are present when fraud occurs*

  *First, there is an **incentive or pressure** that provides a reason to commit fraud.*

*Second, there is an **opportunity** for fraud to be perpetrated (eg. absence of controls, ineffective controls, or the ability of management to override controls.)*

*Third, the individuals committing the fraud possess an attitude that enables them to **rationalize** the fraud" (Wikipedia.org).*

In our application of the fraud triangle, **opportunity** is located at the top of the triangle. **Pressure/motive** is placed at the left base of the triangle. **Rationalization** is found at the right base of the triangle. And while the elements of the triangle are not limited to fraud, they certainly find application in this circumstance.

ELEMENT ONE: OPPORTUNITY

We will resume our examination of Alex's continuing actions, at this point, with the most obvious of the fraud triangle elements—opportunity. Clearly Alex had the opportunity to commit the fraud all along. As the transcript from his testimony at Noel's trial indicates:

> *"As Bryan was becoming more involved with Titan Composites, and he actually moved his office out of the CEP offices to become involved with Titan at their offices, I had to take a more day-to-day role in the business in terms of overseeing the staff and making some of the decisions necessary for operating the business."*

"Opportunity" can be defined as, *"a situation or condition favorable for attainment of a goal"* (Dictionary.com). Within the business functions of Certified Estate Planners, Alex's operational responsibilities were replete with opportunities for the commission of fraud. The opportunities did not suddenly make themselves available. They had always been there. Our reading of the "**Complaint For Permanent Injunction And For Other Relief**" serves to underscore the plethora of opportunities. At some point, as we will learn from his own words, Alex took advantage of those opportunities.

A most critical component of our examination is not whether or not the opportunities were available to enable him to commit the fraud, but rather, that he ultimately did commit the fraud.

Within any organization, there are opportunities for fraudulent undertakings. Ranging from taking a number two lead pencil to selling national security secrets, if an individual's goal is to divert assets to himself there will exist "a situation or condition favorable for attainment of a goal." An individual may work in an organization for ten years and never engage in an illegal act. But on day one of the eleventh year, circumstances can change and the same individual utilizes an opportunity that had been there all along. What happened in Alex's life that released the fraudster that had, seemingly, lain dormant to that point?

Two of the salient, fraud triangle elements—pressure/motive and rationalization—provide a most intriguing focus of our inquiry to understand his behavior.

Element Two: Pressure/Motive

First, let us define some terms:

> "Pressure" is defined as "a moral force that compels" (Dictionary.com).
>
> "Moral force" is defined as "an efficient incentive" (thefreedictionary.com).
>
> "Motive" is defined as "something that causes a person to act in a certain way, do a certain thing" (Dictionary.com).

If we combine the three definitions, to conceptualize pressure/motive, as it relates to fraud, we can develop an operational definition along the line of "an effective incentive that compels a person to behave in a manner consistent with the intention of committing fraud."

An Endless Stream of Lies

The pressure/motive element, as it related to Alex, came forth as he gave testimony during Noel's trial. At this ford in the stream, we will focus on the fraudulent activities related to his stock trading. Alex's stock trading endeavors did not meet with a positive outcome—he was losing significant amounts of money. As the transcript of Alex's testimony reveals:

> *Q. Now, when this stock trading program began to be offered in mid 2002 to CEP clients, how was the trading going?*
> *A. The trading went well until about May or June, and then the trading was not so good after that.*
> *Q. May and June of when?*
> *A. May or June of 2002.*
> *Q. And when you say after June of 2002 it wasn't going so well, what's that mean?*
> *A. It means that losses were being generated. There were some gains that were being generated, but there were more losses that were generated than gains.*
> *Q. So overall, after the summer of 2002, in a given quarter, were the trades net positive or net negative?*
> *A. In most instances they were net negative.*
> *Q. Did you tell the clients about that?*
> *A. No, I did not.*
> *Q. What do you mean by that?*
> *A. The clients did not know that their funds were losing money.*
> *Q. After the midsummer of 2002.*
> *A. Correct.*
> *Q. Well, weren't you keeping clients updated on how their accounts were doing?*
> *A. Yes.*
> *Q. Well, how were clients being kept up to date?*
> *A. They were being kept up to date via quarterly statements that would be sent out.*

Q. Sent out how?
A. Sent out via the Postal Service.
Q. And who was preparing those client reports?
A. I was preparing figures for them, and then they were put into a presentable format by Heather Noel.
Q. And let's take the third quarter of 2002. Was the trading in the third quarter of 2002 a net gain or a net loss?
A. The trading would have been a net loss during that point.
Q. Did you send out client reports showing a loss?
A. No, I did not.
Q. Why not?
A. At that point I hoped that the trading system would turn around and right itself at some point.
Q. Well, why couldn't you tell clients that there had been a loss and just tell them to hang on?
A. I was also not telling Bryan Noel during that time. I was scared to death of the consequences of that getting out to any clients or to him.
Q. Well, what were you concerned would happen if you told Mr. Noel?
A. He's not a man that takes bad news very well, so I was concerned that he might be extremely irritated with such news and that ultimately clients might want to pull their funds out.
Q. Were you concerned about losing your job?
A. I was concerned about that as well.
Q. So just to be clear, at least beginning the third Quarter of 2002, your Pinnacle trading program is losing money.
A. Yes, it is.
Q. And you're lying to clients about that.
A. Yes, I am.
Q. And you're lying to Mr. Noel about that.
A. Yes, I am.
Q. And you're sending false account statements out in the mail.
A. Yes.

An Endless Stream of Lies

Q. At that point, this fraud that you're perpetrating, are you doing that by yourself or with someone else?
A. At that point that was by myself.

Keep in mind that pressure/motive is idiosyncratic. A circumstance (stock results flowing into the negative column at an increasing volume) that may, for one individual, be no more than a "bump in the road of life," may be, for another, perceived as a catastrophic event. According to Alex, the following were the increasingly emerging dynamics:

- Reduction of funds due to his stock trading activities
- Fear of telling clients lest they withdraw their money
- Fear of telling his partner
- The possibility of the loss of his position served as the catalyst (pressure/motive) to set in motion his willingness to falsify the quarterly reports

Changing circumstances can serve to reveal a different nature (side) of an individual—a nature of the individual having lain dormant to that point.

Sir Francis Bacon (1561–1626) was a prolific and insightful writer. He was a man ahead of his time. One of Bacon's treatises, "Of Nature in Men," is worth our review and application to Alex:

> "Like as it was with AEsop's damsel, turned from a cat to a woman, who sat very demutely at the board's end, till a mouse ran before her. Therefore, let a man either avoid the occasion altogether; or put himself often to it, that he may be little moved with it. A man's nature is best perceived in privateness, for there is no affectation; in passion, for that putteth a man out of his precepts; and in a new case or experiment, for there custom leaveth him."

Hundreds of years before Dr. Donald Cressey put forth his theory with regard to the fraud triangle, Bacon had addressed the pressure/motive element most succinctly. In the above quote, Bacon is telling us that circumstances (pressure/motive) "putteth a man out of his precepts"—meaning that circumstances, especially new circumstances (consistent losses in the stock market for example), can serve to reveal a dimension of the person that had heretofore not been made manifest. Pressure/motive does not create a fraudster but rather reveals the fraudster that has been within all along. It is interesting to note that, after falling into debt, Bacon himself was convicted of taking bribes. Apparently, for Bacon, debt did indeed "put him out of his precepts." Oh well.

In Robert Louis Stevenson's (1850–1894) *The Strange Case of Dr. Jekyll and Mr. Hyde*, Doctor Jekyll provides a telling account of his transformation and actions. Within the narrative, he reveals:

> "The drug had no discriminating action; it was neither diabolical nor divine; it but shook the doors of the prisonhouse of my disposition; and like the captives of Philippi, that which stood within ran forth. At that time my virtue slumbered; my evil, kept awake by ambition, was alert and swift to seize the occasion; and the thing that was projected was Edward Hyde. Hence, although I had now two characters as well as two appearances, one was wholly evil, and the other was still the old Henry Jekyll, that incongruous compound of whose reformation and improvement I had already learned to despair. The movement was thus wholly toward the worse."

The drug did not turn Doctor Jekyll into the evil being into which he transformed; rather, it released the being that was waiting patiently all along in the anteroom of his heart.

With my profound apologies to Mr. Stephenson, let's take license to make a couple of wording modifications in his account, as if the character were Alex, and not Doctor Jekyll, to illustrate our point:

An Endless Stream of Lies

> "*The **losses (that) were being generated** had no discriminating action; it was neither diabolical nor divine; it but shook the doors of the prisonhouse of my disposition; and like the captives of Philippi, that which stood within ran forth. At that time my virtue slumbered; my evil, kept awake by ambition, was alert and swift to seize the **opportunity**; and the thing that was projected was **Alex Klosek the fraudster**. Hence, although I had now two characters as well as two appearances, one was wholly evil, and the other was still the old **Alex Klosek**, that incongruous compound of whose reformation and improvement I had already learned to despair. The movement was thus wholly toward the worse.*"

At this point, opportunity was now added to pressure/motive. Two of the three requisites for fraud as presented by Dr. Cressey were now in place.

Pausing for a moment, we have more to explore regarding this pressure/motive dynamic before we travel further downstream, past Alex's stock trading, financial evaporations of the investors' resources, to his rationalization. First, it is necessary to go back up stream to find the source of Alex—who had no real life experience trading stocks—having become involved in such a financially perilous undertaking. How did Alex become involved in trading stocks? Once more we look to his testimony.

> *Q. Now, as of early and mid 2001 when you moved over to CEP from One-to-One Wireless, did Mr. Noel know anything about this trading program that you had developed in college?*
> *A. Not at that time.*
> *Q. Directing your attention to the fall of 2001, did that change?*
> *A. Yes, it did.*
> *Q. Can you tell the jury what happened in the fall of 2001?*
> *A. In the fall of 2001—we had the September 11th attacks in 2001. Bryan knew I had an interest in the markets, and his accounts had taken a substantial hit since the 2000 stock market decline, so at that*

point I took over the management of his personal account in terms of logging in and making stock trades.

Q. Well, what was it that caused Mr. Noel to have you start engaging in his trading in the fall of 2001? Did you tell him something?

A. Yes.

Q. What did you tell him?

A. I had told him about the system that — — — — and I had developed.

Q. So Mr. Noel gave you access to his personal trading accounts?

A. Yes, he did.

Q. And at that time, approximately how much money was in those personal trading accounts that you were managing?

A. I do not recall the exact figures, but it was somewhere in the 10 to 12,000 vicinity.

Q. 10 to $12,000?

A. Yes, 10 to $12,000.

Q. Did you trade those monies?

A. Yes, I did.

Q. Did you use that program you developed in college?

A. Yes, I did.

Q. Is this the first time you had ever used real money for that program?

A. Yes, it was.

Q. How did it go?

A. It went pretty well for 2001 and early 2002.

Q. When you say "pretty well," what do you mean?

A. The returns that it produced were something on the order of 20 to 25 percent annualized.

Q. And this was from sometime after September 11th, 2001, you said, through 2002?

A. Yes, it was.

Q. And when in 2002? How long did you keep doing that?

A. 2002, probably about May.

Q. At some point you have a discussion with Mr. Noel about whether others could be offered these trading services.
A. Yes, we did.
Q. When was that?
A. That would have been sometime in early 2002.
Q. Tell the jury about that.
A. Bryan was impressed with the results that were generated in late 2001, Bryan Noel, and he said this could be something that could be offered to the existing CEP clients that we had.
Q. Only the existing clients?
A. It could be offered to new clients as well.
Q. And so was the decision made?
A. Yes, it was.
Q. And what was the decision?
A. The decision was made to make this available to new and existing clients.
Q. To make what available?
A. To make this trading system available.
Q. Were clients going to be told about this trading system?
A. Yes, they would be.
Q. What—was there a decision made about what type detail was going to be provided to them about the trading system?
A. That would be a system that does involve day-trading and invests all the funds in stocks.
Q. What—when you say "all the funds," what funds were supposed to be invested in the stock market?
A. Any incoming client funds that were designated as such for that type of trading.
Q. And were funds that were designated as such put in a particular account?
A. Yes, they were.
Q. And what account was that?

A. They would have been put into Pinnacle's bank account and, ultimately, broker's account.

Q. So prior to early 2002, you said that Pinnacle was not involved in money management?

A. That is correct.

Q. But after early 2002, was Pinnacle involved in money management?

A. Yes, it was.

Q. And based on your discussion with Mr. Noel, what were clients told about how those Pinnacle funds were going to be managed after early 2002?

A. Those investors would have been told that they were being used for a relatively rapid day-trading system and that all of those funds would be invested in the stock market.

Q. Now, who was going to be out there promoting this program to clients?

A. That would have been Bryan Noel and the other sales staff.

Q. And was the other sales staff told about the trading program as well?

A. Yes, they were.

Now, we have discovered that the source for the stock trading tributary was Alex and not Bryan Noel. Alex was the one who "had an interest in the markets." It was Alex who "told" Noel about the stock trading system that he had helped to developed in college. It was Alex that "took over the management of" Noel's personal account. Verbs are telling in that they show action or state of being. Alex:

- Had an interest
- Told Noel
- Took over

Acting upon his market interest, Alex approached Noel and told him of his stock trading system.

As a result of that conversation, Alex took over. From Noel's relatively small, personal investment, the trickle grew significantly into a raging river of investors' money that ultimately evaporated, leaving over one hundred people high and dry.

ELEMENT THREE: RATIONALIZATION

"Rationalization" can be defined, "To ascribe one's acts to causes that superficially seem reasonable and valid but that actually are unrelated to the true, possibly unconscious and often less creditable or agreeable causes" (Dictionary.com).

In Shakespeare's tragedy *Othello*, there is a forceful example of rationalization. Othello had murdered his wife, Desdemona, as well as his loyal friend, Cassio. He committed these murders in an act of (unwarranted) jealousy. In the play, Lodovico asks the following:

> *"O thou Othello, thou wert once so good,*
> *Fall'n in the practise of a damned slave,*
> *What shall be said to thee?"*

Othello replies:

> *"Why, any thing:*
> *An honourable murderer, if you will;*
> *For nought I did in hate, but all in honour"*

The act of rationalization allowed Othello to attribute what he had done as an act of honor rather than a needless reaction of a jealous husband. Honor "seemed reasonable and valid," whereas the more truthful "suspicion and distrust" lacked the nobility of the former.

Alex and the Fraud Triangle

While Alex was testifying, a question opened the door, allowing Alex to articulate his rationalization for his fraudulent behavior.

> *Q. What was going on in 2003 that would cause you to do something like this?*
> *A. There were many circumstances in 2003, especially the latter part of the year where I had a bad breakup with an ex-girlfriend and I started drinking heavily, started smoking marijuana at some points from 2003 to 2004, and also even engaging in sexual activity at that time that I was hiding from my parents. Hiding many of those things from my parents.*

As with Othello, our analysis of Alex's words is most revealing. First, we have to put his response in context: Back to the question asked, "What was going on in 2003 that would cause you to do something like this?" We know "what was going on" as articulated by Alex, the pressure/motive of:

- Stock losses
- Fear of telling clients, lest they withdraw their money
- Fear of telling his partner
- Loss of position

Now, as to regarding the "cause," i.e., rationalization for sending out false reports, Alex responded:

Bad breakup with a girlfriend resulting in:
- Drinking heavily
- Smoking marijuana
- Engaging in sexual activity hidden from his parents.

The juxtaposition of pressure/motive with rationalization forms an "If–Then" logic operation. Keep in mind that it is an idiosyncratic logic

43

operation. Consequently, in Alex's world, as he articulates it and we endeavor to understand it:

> **IF** someone is under pressure because of stock trading losses and fear of clients, partner and loss of position,
>
> **AND** subsequently there is a breakup in a relationship leading to drinking heavily, smoking marijuana and sexual activity unknown to parents,
>
> **THEN** the fraud becomes the optimal choice.

It is not necessary to agree with Alex's articulation of his reality. It is only necessary to understand that it *is* Alex's articulation of how things "operate" in his world.

Comparing Alex and the fraud triangle to the classic fire triangle (fuel, heat and oxygen), we find that the stock trading opportunity constituted the fuel, his articulated pressure/motive was the heat and his rationalization supplied the oxygen. Figuratively speaking, there was, at this point, fire on the water.

Thoughts, Comments and Analysis

What are your impressions, to this point, with regard to this circumstance?

Exactly what do you know?

What is it that you **know** that you don't know?

What questions would you ask in order to know?

What steps would you take in order to know?

Points to Ponder

At another point in Alex's testimony we read the following possible motivation for falsifying the account statements:

> Q. And what were you going to do with regard to account statements after this meeting for clients?
> A. There would be nothing different than what had previously been done.
> Q. Which was what?
> A. Which was showing them rates of return above two and a half percent per quarter.
> Q. And the two and a half percent was a significant number why?
> A. That was significant because that was the figure that was in the membership application that clients signed, when they came in to become clients, stating that no fees would be taken for any performance figure below that.

01. What does the sentence "There would be nothing different than what had previously been done" bring to mind?

02. What does the use of the word "*taken*" found in "no fees would be taken for any performance figure below that" bring to mind?

03. Does falsifying the two and a half percent return to clients illustrate pressure/motive, opportunity, rationalization or something else?

04. What questions would you pose to Alex at this point?

Alex and the Fraud Triangle

Content – Context Application

A district supervisor with the Division of Motor Vehicle License and Theft Bureau was charged with stealing property and misconduct in office. The warrant indicated the supervisor had bought stolen property—three stolen lawn mowers—that were part of an ongoing investigation. The warrant also stated he subsequently concealed the evidence and hindered the investigation into those who were involved in the theft.

In regard to an individual holding a supervisory position in an investigative agency:

01. Would the purchase of three stolen lawn mowers (part of an ongoing investigation) be a function of pressure/motive, rationalization or opportunity?

02. Would concealing the evidence and hindering the investigation be a function of either of the same three fraud triangle elements?

03. Why would someone functioning within an organization that consistently discovers and prosecutes violators of the law believe that they would be able to successfully prevail?

04. What questions would you pose to this individual?

CHAPTER FOUR

Alex Met the Investors at the Well He Took Their Water and the Well Ran Dry

From reveries so airy, from the toil
Of dropping buckets into empty wells,
And growing old in drawing nothing up.
—William Cowper (1731–1800), English Poet

Navigation Point and Heading → Let's walk up another tributary, just a bit, to take a close look at Alex's involvement with the CEP sales presentations and his meetings with individual prospective clients. He has admitted that from 2002 until 2006, he was sending out false financial reports, deceiving not only the clients, but his partner, Bryan Noel, as well. Concurrently, with the stock trading, financial losses and the falsified financial reports, sales presentations designed to acquire additional investors were ongoing. While the presentations were being conducted and during the subsequent follow-up meetings with potential investors, only one person in the room knew the funds were diminishing and the financial reports were false. That one person was Alex.

49

An Endless Stream of Lies

Nothing Happens until Somebody Makes a Sale

During Noel's trial, Alex provided testimony with regard to the marketing and sales endeavors of Certified Estate Planners:

> *Q. Did you have the opportunity to observe any of these sales presentations?*
> *A. Yes, I did.*
> *Q. How would these—where would these sales presentations occur?*
> *A. These sales presentations would typically occur at restaurants in the Hendersonville area, such as Hubert's or Blackwater Grill or McGuffy's.*
> *Q. And how was it that clients were invited to attend these sales presentations?*
> *A. There were mailings that were done to prospective clients, inviting them to attend the sales presentation.*
> *Q. Have you ever seen any of the brochures?*
> *A. Yes, I have.*
> *Q. Let me show you Government Exhibit 20A, which is already in evidence, and ask if you've seen it before.*
> *A. Yes, I have.*
> *Q. What is that?*
> *A. That is a seminar brochure for CEP.*
> *Q. And is this one of the brochures that was sent out to invite clients to the seminars?*
> *A. Yes, it was.*
> *Q. Can you tell the jury what these seminars were like.*
> *A. These seminars basically consisted of a sales presentation that involved the four-corners' approach to estate planning, which is basically investments, legal, taxes, and insurance. Anybody that was interested would then fill out a form saying that they were interested and requested an appointment to discuss this further.*
> *Q. Was any type of meal offered?*

A. Yes. A free meal was offered.

Q. Were clients told about any investment strategies at these seminars?

A. They were not told specific investment strategies.

Q. Did that come later?

A. Yes, it did.

Q. Who would be the presenter at these seminars?

A. Bryan Noel was the presenter at the seminars.

Q. Did anybody else speak?

A. Yes, there typically would be some other speakers.

Q. Were you ever the speaker?

A. I was not the speaker, but I was present for many of the seminars in a supportive and administrative role.

Q. Why didn't you speak?

A. I'm not really much of a salesman.

Q. So why were you there?

A. I was there to show the investors, potential investors—to give kind of a face to the strategy that was going on at CEP, so that they could see everybody that was involved.

Q. When you say give a face to the strategy, what was the strategy?

A. The strategy would be to ultimately tell them about any potential investments that could be made in Pinnacle.

Q. When clients were advised as to how their funds were being invested, what were they told?

A. They were told those funds were being invested in stocks.

Q. And, specifically, those were the Pinnacle funds?

A. Yes.

Q. Is that what clients were consistently told?

A. Yes, it was.

Q. Now, after the seminars, were there any follow-up meetings with potential clients?

A. Yes, there were.

Q. And can you tell the jury about that?

A. Those meetings would be done at the offices of CEP, where, basically, the clients would be given a further presentation. At that point they would be told about the potential for investment with Pinnacle, and then they could make a decision as to whether they wanted to do business or not.

Q. Who would conduct these private meetings at the offices of CEP?

A. Most of the time those were conducted by Bryan Noel.

Q. Anybody else?

A. Yes, there were.

Q. Who else?

A. Some of the other sales staff would be involved with those meetings as well, and I would be present for some of the meetings in a support role.

Q. What do you mean you were there in a support role?

A. For clients that may have had questions about the strategy, the trading strategy, I would be available to answer those questions.

Q. And did you at times meet with clients?

A. Yes, I did.

Q. Did you tell them about the stock-trading program?

A. Yes, I did.

Q. Did you ever have clients come up to your office and look at your trading system?

A. Yes, I did.

Q. Did you ever meet with clients in these private consultations by yourself?

A. The initial consultations?

Q. Right.

A. No, I did not.

Q. Why not?
A. It was necessary to have somebody that could put together the full estate plan. Basically, what I knew about their estate plan would be the taxation aspect as well as the trading aspect.

Q. In 2004, even in late 2004, are you conducting private client consultations for potential investors in CEP?
A. There were some contacts that I had with clients, but at that point it would typically involve the sales staff making presentations to them.

Q. In 2005, are you doing private consultations with potential CEP clients?
A. In 2005, there were one or two clients that were referrals from existing clients that I did have initial contact with, but I did not have contact with new clients that were coming in without any familiarity with the business.

WELLS

In past times, water wells served a multitude of societal purposes and were of significant importance. As an example, after over two hundred years, the old well at the University of North Carolina at Chapel Hill holds a place of prominence and esteem for faculty, students and alumni. Pictures dating from over a hundred years old to today show people standing, socializing and interacting with one another at the old well site.

Aside from the obvious functioning of a well—a source of water—it also operated as the information-exchange device of the day. People of the time could meet face to face, barter, buy, sell, exchange news and information, and interact as members of a society. In the Bible, John 4, there is a classic example of the multi-functionality of a well through which we can examine the actions of Alex and his partner to obtain investors:

John 4: "*So He came to a city of Samaria called Sychar, near the parcel of ground that Jacob gave to his son Joseph; ⁶and Jacob's well was there. So Jesus, being wearied from His journey, was sitting thus by the well. It was about the sixth hour.*

⁷There came a woman of Samaria to draw water. Jesus said to her, "Give Me a drink." ⁸For His disciples had gone away into the city to buy food. ⁹Therefore the Samaritan woman said to Him, "How is it that You, being a Jew, ask me for a drink since I am a Samaritan woman?" (For Jews have no dealings with Samaritans.) ¹⁰Jesus answered and said to her, "If you knew the gift of God, and who it is who says to you, 'Give Me a drink,' you would have asked Him, and He would have given you living water." ¹¹She said to Him, "Sir, You have nothing to draw with and the well is deep; where then do You get that living water? ¹²You are not greater than our father Jacob, are You, who gave us the well, and drank of it himself and his sons and his cattle?" ¹³Jesus answered and said to her, "Everyone who drinks of this water will thirst again; ¹⁴but whoever drinks of the water that I will give him shall never thirst; but the water that I will give him will become in him a well of water springing up to eternal life."

¹⁵The woman said to Him, "Sir, give me this water, so I will not be thirsty nor come all the way here to draw." ¹⁶He said to her, "Go, call your husband and come here." ¹⁷The woman answered and said, "I have no husband." Jesus said to her, "You have correctly said, 'I have no husband'; ¹⁸for you have had five husbands, and the one whom you now have is not your husband; this you have said truly." ¹⁹The woman said to Him, "Sir, I perceive that You are a prophet."

²⁸So the woman left her waterpot, and went into the city and said to the men, ²⁹"Come, see a man who told me all the things that I have done; this is not the Christ, is it?" ³⁰They went out of the city, and were coming to Him.

Alex Met the Investors at the Well

39 From that city many of the Samaritans believed in Him because of the word of the woman who testified, "He told me all the things that I have done." 41 Many more believed because of His word."

Jesus used his encounter with the woman to offer her the opportunity to make a decision that would change her life. How does the narrative of the meeting at the well relate to the fraudulent actions of Alex and his partner, Bryan Noel? They too needed a gathering place where they could interact and endeavor to convince people to invest in Certified Estate Planners.

Rather than a well, as Alex testified, CEP's sales presentations would "typically occur at restaurants in the Hendersonville area, such as Hubert's or Blackwater Grill or McGuffy's." Additionally, their presentations at the restaurants were such that "[a] free meal was offered." They utilized a myriad of methodologies for drawing attention to their investment proposition—"flyers, conferences and via their website" ("Complaint For Permanent Injunction And For Other Relief," #20). The sales presentation tactics of Jesus with the woman at the well and CEP's presentations with the potential investors were tactically similar with a comparable goal—have the individual to "make a decision." CEP's "seminars basically consisted of a sales presentation that involved the four-corners' approach." Tactical similarities aside, the purposes of their encounters were polar opposites—one sales presentation was designed to give, and the other sales presentation was ultimately destined to take.

Tales

CEP's goal was also to get people to believe and to act on that belief. Just as importantly, CEP hoped that current investors would in turn "bring in" other investors by sharing the good news. But CEP also had a gap that they had to overcome—a gap between people having money and those same people deciding to entrust their money to CEP.

CEP was actively involved in marketing. The targets were "primarily wealthy, elderly customers." The marketing "advertisements falsely claimed that the customers would be able to avoid their income taxes by placing their assets in trust while still continuing to 'manag[e] everything' but 'own nothing'" (20). So, the complexity of CEP's sales presentations' deception increased exponentially. Not only are the sales presentation claims regarding the avoidance of taxes false, but the report of the financial health of CEP itself is a fabrication.

Jesus was handling his marketing directly. CEP had a multi-faceted approach. The goals, however, were the same: to draw people in, conduct the presentation and cause a positive response on the part of the individual. Jesus wanted to offer something to the person freely, that would flow continually. CEP wanted the person to initially entrust them with his or her money. They declared that they would, in turn, multiply that investment into an endless stream of revenue. Jesus turned water into wine. Conversely, CEP turned their client's liquidity into dust. Jesus fed the multitude with just a few loaves of bread and a couple of fish. The few in CEP devoured that which had belonged to the multitude.

As reported in the *Henderson Time News*, August 11, 2006, in an article titled "Nervous Investors Consider Restitution Plots," one investor reported that ". . . he invested a 'substantial' amount of money with the business over the last two years. He said he dealt primarily with Alex Klosek, who acted as a trustee in taking his money and placing it into investments." Another ". . . invested $200,000 of her retirement savings" with CEP. Also, in the *Henderson Times-News*, February 20, 2010, in an article titled "Noel's Victims Focus of Testimony," still another investor testified at the trial that ". . . she and her husband not only invested with CEP, but also put $50,000 into Noel's startups International Mineral Exchange and later Titan Composites." Two other investors who collectively lost $194,000 testified at the trial with regard to their losses.

"And then they could make a decision"

People make decisions throughout the day. They have to decide when to get out of bed, what to wear, what to eat, where to go, and what to do. Influencing another person's cognition toward a predetermined outcome—persuasion—is an art. A criterion for success is the ability to affect the nervous system of others on a continuing basis. While that statement may sound a bit Machiavellian, if a car salesperson cannot persuade people on a regular basis to purchase a car, then the dealership will soon replace him with someone who can. If a supervisor cannot motivate the division personnel to more excellent productivity, then she will most likely find herself out on the street.

People make decisions continually, and they make those decisions on the self-interest principle. We select what we believe is the best watermelon in the bin, the best spouse with whom to share a life, the best home for our family and the best investment vehicle for our money.

All of CEP's sales presentation endeavors were designed to convince others that entrusting them with their money was the best investment they could make with their money.

CEP had also endeavored to get people to "believe." Those people believed to the point that they collectively turned over more than seven million dollars of their money to those who had made a presentation. However, just as with Jesus' proposal, not everyone believed. In the previously referenced *Henderson Times-News* article of August 11, 2006, a certified financial planner noted, "I recommended several of my clients not to go there, because I questioned the return on the yields that were being promised. People get fliers to go to these seminars and if it sounds too good to be true, it probably is."

Ultimately, to paraphrase the writings of the poet William Cowper, found in this chapter heading, over one hundred trusting investors would find themselves dropping their buckets into the empty CEP well. A well that had been drained dry by those who had undertaken to first gain trust and then betray that trust in the extreme. Gaining trust is a process that, in and of itself, makes no distinction as to the wisdom of placing trust in those who would seek to have it. Rather, it is the motive of the heart (good versus evil, give versus take) within those who would win the minds and hearts of others that is the distinguishing factor.

57

During the trial, when Alex was questioned as to the terminology regarding taking other investors' money and making payment to still other investors, the following transpired:

> Q. *What's that called?*
> A. *That's called a Ponzi scheme.*

NOTE: What is a Ponzi scheme? "A Ponzi scheme is a fraudulent, investment operation that pays returns to separate investors, not from any actual profit earned by the organization, but from their own money or money paid by subsequent investors" (http://en.wikipedia.org/wiki/Ponzi_scheme).

THOUGHTS, COMMENTS AND ANALYSIS

What are your impressions, to this point, with regard to this circumstance?

Exactly what do you know?

What is it that you **know** that you don't know?

What questions would you ask in order to know?

What steps would you take in order to know?

Points to Ponder

In other portions of his testimony, Alex described meetings of another sort. The initial meetings, addressed in this chapter, were designed to *obtain* clients. In the following, Alex explains the meetings that we designed to *retain* clients as the evaporation of funds become more dramatic.

> Q. Let me show you Government Exhibit 8HH, which I believe is already in evidence, and ask you if you recognize that.
> A. Yes, I do.
> Q. What is 8HH?
> A. That is a letter that was sent to the clients of Certified Estate Planners by me.
> Q. What's the date of the letter?
> A. The date is February 9th, 2006.
> Q. Why did you send this letter?
> A. Because of large withdrawals that were made by the Fishers and other clients, as we had previously mentioned with the Fishers. There was an effort made to try to hold on to some of those funds longer so that maybe something could be salvaged and the client would not take their funds elsewhere.
> Q. Whose idea was that?
> A. That was an idea that was discussed between Bryan and me.
> Q. Is Mr. Noel referenced on this letter's attachment?
> A. Yes, he is.

Q. And what does it say?
A. It says that "Should you wish to close an account, an additional procedure will apply. In addition to having the Request for Trustee Minutes signed by you, Bryan Noel will meet with you personally for a final meeting."
Q. What was the purpose of that?
A. The purpose of that meeting was to try to salvage that client and hopefully retain the funds within Pinnacle.
Q. Who was going to meet with the clients to try to keep their funds at Pinnacle?
A. That would be Bryan. I would probably be in that meeting as well.
Q. Well, why does it say Bryan? What's the purpose of having Bryan at that meeting?
A. Bryan was much better at being persuasive in his sales abilities than I was.
Q. Why did you need to keep the funds of clients at Pinnacle? What was the concern?
A. The concern was that if they withdrew those that it would further hinder any efforts to try to trade those funds or try to get something back from Titan.
Q. As of February 2006, if clients started withdrawing their funds, were there sufficient funds to give back to clients?
A. There were not.
Q. Who knew that?
A. Bryan Noel and I knew that.

01. What differences, if any, do you see as to the mindsets of those responsible for conducting the meeting between the *obtain-purposed* meeting and the *retain-purposed* meetings?

02. What differences, if any, do you see as to the mindsets of the clients between the *obtain-purposed* meeting and the *retain-purposed meeting*?

03. Would these two meetings require different sales presentations dynamics?

04. What questions would you pose to Alex at this point?

Content – Context Application

A former lieutenant for a sheriff's department was indicted on sixty counts of fraudulent billing for work while he was off duty. The indictment indicated that he was being paid for being at work in two places at the same time on sixty occasions during a two year period.

01. What were the "trust issues" that had to be formulated by this lieutenant within the sheriff's department?

02. What were the "trust issues" that had to be formulated by this lieutenant within the organizations that were the source of his secondary employment?

03. What are the ramifications when those placed in positions of trust, such as law enforcement, educators, medical professionals, etc., violate that trust?

04. What question would you pose to this individual?

CHAPTER FIVE

The River Turns and Turns Once Again
Alex Leaks to the FBI
Alex's Double Knavery

Let me see now:
To get his place and to plume up my will
In double knavery — How, how? Let's see
    OTHELLO, ACT I, SCENE III

NAVIGATION POINT AND HEADING → Matters have deteriorated to the point it has become necessary to have meetings in order to retain clients and, more especially, their monies. Alex has previously been submitting false financial statements, keeping both the clients and his partner in the dark. Desperate times call for desperate measures. Decisions have to be made. Actions have to be taken. For Alex, navigation is becoming increasingly difficult.

SOMETHING MUST BE DONE

In June of 2006, Alex made the decision to speak with agents from the Federal Bureau of Investigation. It was shortly after that meeting with the federal representatives that Alex made his initial request to meet with me for lunch. He had charted his course most carefully, as he said in his testimony at Noel's trial:

> Q. Directing your attention to June of 2006, specifically June 30th, did something significant happen that day?
> A. Yes, it did.
> Q. And what's that?
> A. I had my first meeting with the FBI.
> Q. What do you mean by that?
> A. I had—in about May of 2006, it was getting to the point where the funds had dwindled, there were so many lies that were going on with CEP and Pinnacle and Titan and everything else, and I could not keep up the show game, so I realized that something had to be done. And then my wife also told me at that time if we don't do—
> Q. Don't tell us what your wife said. Just talk about what you did.
> A. That we would need to do something because the ultimate result would be that everything would fall upon me. So I searched out attorneys and, ultimately, in June of 2006 had my first meeting with the FBI on June 30th.
> Q. I don't want you to talk about anything you talked about with your attorneys. How was it that you ended up at the FBI offices?
> A. There was one that—one particular attorney that knew somebody that had contact, and that's how I ended up getting in there.
> Q. So you didn't just, like, wander in one day.
> A. No, I did not just wander in.
> Q. Did you have an appointment?
> A. Yes, I did.
> Q. Who did you meet with?
> A. I met with Drew Grafton.
> Q. What was the date of that meeting?
> A. The date of that meeting was June 30, 2006.
> Q. What did you do during that meeting?

The River Turns and Turns Once Again

> *A. During that meeting I started to outline some of what had happened with him and give him the story about CEP.*
> *Q. And when you say "him," who are you referring to?*
> *A. To Drew Grafton.*

Why had Alex reached a point wherein he decided the verbs "searched," "knew," and "had contact" were necessary? Had he had a change of heart? Was there, for him, a crisis of conscience, a realization that his past acts—falsifying reports, deceiving and taking what did not belong to him—were wrong? In the dead of the night, did some still, small voice whisper convincingly to him? Did he ever indicate he was motivated by a feeling of remorse to finally do the right thing? Certainly, that mindset does not appear to be the case.

Remember, Alex testified:

> *A. That we would need to do something because the ultimate result would be that everything would fall upon me.*

A close examination of Alex's choice of words proves most revealing. Each of Alex's words is a subjective choice. Subjective word choice is a form of behavior, and that behavior is a function of the premeditated goal of the speaker (or writer in the case of a written narrative or account). By our examination of Alex's word choice, we gain insight into Alex's cognitions and consequently, his ultimate goal:

> *A. I had—in about May of 2006, it was getting to the point where the funds had dwindled, there were so many lies that were going on with CEP and Pinnacle and Titan and everything else, and I could not keep up the show game, so I realized that something had to be done.*

First, what was it about the "dwindled" funds specifically at this point? As far back as June of 2002, Alex's stock trading endeavors were resulting in a loss (dwindling) of funds. By his own admission, Alex testified that he deceived Noel and the CEP clients, and was falsifying quarterly reports. He had continued to deceive Noel, up to a point, and send out falsified quarterly reports.

So, according to Alex, his motivation for going to the FBI was that he could not "keep up the show game." We always pay attention to the terms that someone uses to frame a circumstance or a situation. What might Alex's utilization of the term "show game" imply?

There were additional pressure/motives acting upon Alex to take action as shown by his testimony:

> Q. Okay. We're using two — "loan" twice here. Who is getting the bridge loan?
> A. IME would be getting the bridge loan.
> Q. And what was IME supposed to do with the funds that it got from the bridge loan?
> A. The funds would be used to repay the loan from Pinnacle to IME.
> Q. The $2 million?
> A. The $2 million.
> Q. At this point, in February of 2004, is there any documentation for this $2 million loan to IME?
> A. There was not.
>
> ---
>
> Q. Was that $2 million transfer of funds to IME from Pinnacle investor funds the last time that Pinnacle Investor funds were transferred to IME?
> A. No, it was not.
> Q. Were the other transfers supported by and authorized By debentures?
> A. No, not all of them were.

The River Turns and Turns Once Again

> *Q. Approximately how much additional money was Transferred to IME that was not authorized by specific debentures?*
> *A. Approximately another $2 million.*
> *Q. Another $2 million in addition to the 2 million in December of 2003?*
> *A. Yes.*

As noted above, Alex testified that Noel had borrowed at least four million dollars from Certified Estate Planners. The funds were for Noel's startup companies. In addition to the stock losses and the borrowed money—as cited in the September 2007 "Complaint For Permanent Injunction And For Other Relief"—Alex and Noel were both withdrawing unmerited, large, account management fees. How much were those fees? Alex provided the amount in his testimony:

> *Q. During your time at CEP and Pinnacle, were you getting paid?*
> *A. Yes, I was.*
> *Q. How much were you being paid?*
> *A. I don't remember the exact figure, but I would approximate about 75,000 per year.*
> *Q. 75,000 a year?*
> *A. Yes.*

In short, the liquidity was drying up.

Once the fund level sank to this level, in Alex's mind, matters had to be taken in hand. According to Alex's testimony:

> *Q. Now, in this month of October of 2005, did you have a conversation with Mr. Noel?*
> *A. Yes, I did.*
> *Q. And what was that conversation about in October of 2005?*
> *A. That conversation was about revealing to him some of the extent of the trading losses that were suffered.*

69

Q. Up to this point in October of 2005, had Pinnacle been having trading gains or trading losses on a quarterly basis?
A. For most quarters, it would have been trading losses.
Q. Had you been telling Mr. Noel about the trading losses up through October of 2005?
A. I had not been.
Q. You had not been?
A. I had not been.
Q. Had you been telling clients about the trading losses up to October of 2005?
A. No, I had not.
Q. Did something change in October of 2005?
A. Yes, it did.
Q. What's that?
A. There were some serious losses that were generated during the course of that summer, and I felt that I needed to let Bryan know the extent of the situation.

Q. Was this a problem?
A. Yes.
Q. Why was it a problem?
A. Because of the losses that had been generated because the Titan funds were no longer — the funds that had been lent to Titan were no longer there. This represented a substantial portion of the assets that remained.
Q. So by this point, about how much money had been sent off to IME and Titan?
A. Well, I don't recall the exact figures. It would have been at least 2 and a half to $3 million.

Q. Now, when you — you told Mr. Noel at that point what had occurred?

A. I had told him that there had been significant losses that occurred.
Q. Did you tell him the full story about the losses?
A. I did not.
Q. What do you mean by that?
A. I made it sound like more recent market events that caused this as opposed to something that was ongoing back to 2002.
Q. So you didn't tell him you'd been losing money since 2002?
A. No, I did not.
Q. But you told him you'd lost money.
A. Yes.
Q. Did you tell him how much you had lost?
A. I do not recall if I told him the exact figures.

Motivations Promote Actions

To Alex, there were two activating criteria in play at this point in time:

First, Alex testified, "I felt that I needed to let Bryan know . . ." Alex did not say, "Bryan needed to know," but rather, ". . . *I needed* to let Bryan know . . ." Informing Bryan was an action designed to fulfill a need within Alex, not to resolve a need that was within Bryan. Letting Bryan know that the funds were dwindling met an "Alex need." What was that need?

Secondly, some of the clients wanted to withdraw their money. Alex knew for a certainty that Certified Estate Planners did not have sufficient funds to cover a significant "run" on the funds, and that he had been falsifying quarterly reports and submitting them time and time again.

Bryan's borrowing funds notwithstanding, Alex was the one who had been sending out the falsified reports. Alex was the one losing money over a period of years. At this point, with regard to the continual losses and the falsified quarterly reports, Noel had plausible deniability. Alex obviously knew three things that his partner did not:

- He had been losing money for years
- The quarterly reports were false

- The clients were, literally and figuratively, "at the door"

In October of 2005, Alex made the first move he needed to make. He made Bryan (partially) aware of the fact there were losses. Now, there was a shared, dark knowledge between him and Bryan. In May, of the following year, he would make another move.

For Alex, the realization that informing Bryan was in and of itself not enough became the tipping point at which an additional move must be undertaken. Alex's term, "something," indicates a range of actions for consideration. Whatever that range or action constituted in his mind, the most viable option was to seek out an attorney. However, not just any attorney would suffice. It would need to be an attorney that "had contacts."

To Alex, this was something that "had to be done." Herein, the operative word is "had." With this word, we see the criticality of the need for more action in Alex's mind. Inaction now was not an option—"*Something had to be done.*"

Alex acted in the self-interest principle. His resulting actions—going to the FBI—were the result of his deliberations on the range of "something" and his motivation, brought on by the multiplying effect of "had."

Acting on the self-interest principle is not in and of itself a negative action. Only if the consequences of those actions are detrimental to others do we see self-interest in a disapproving light. As noted previously, people buy the car they believe is best for them; we do not seek out someone who will make us miserable for the rest of our lives as a marriage partner; when grocery shopping we pick out the best fruit or vegetable in the bin. In like manner, we invest our money in a method and with those we believe will provide us the safest, as well as the greatest, return on our investment.

His words continue with, "I would need to do something . . ." In his mind there was no choice. His use of the word "need" makes clear that the circumstances required action on his part and his best choice was to obtain an attorney with contacts. So now our examination is not of the "what" to do, but rather the "why." Alex addresses the "why" most succinctly, ". . . or everything was going to fall on me." Obviously neither of the options—going to the FBI with the revelations or having everything fall on him—would result in a positive outcome. But having everything fall on him was, in his mind, the most negative outcome of the two.

In psychology, this concept is known as an "avoidance-avoidance conflict." Conflict is defined, "Any situation in which there are mutually antagonistic events, motives, purposes, behaviors, impulses, etc." (*The Penguin Dictionary of Psychology*). An avoidance-avoidance conflict is defined, "A conflict resulting from being repelled by two undesirable goals when there are strong pressures to choose one or the other. It is a particularly unpleasant situation which prompts one to select the 'lesser of the two evils'" (*The Penguin Dictionary of Psychology*).

Therefore, he undertook the steps toward the option which in his mind was the "lesser of the two evils." He went to the FBI.

Now, whatever the term "everything" constituted in Alex's mind, it was for him the worst case scenario. "Everything" was worse than going to the FBI. If the house of cards was going to fall, he did not want it all (everything) to "fall" on him. It would be preferable to have the house fall on more than just him. Maybe the majority of the house could fall on someone else. Better still, could there be a way to have the house not fall on him at all?

The pronoun "me" is the most intimate of all the pronouns. It tends to be the recipient of the action of the verb—"fall on me." Once again Alex is operating out of the self-interest principle. But the depth of Alex's self-interest went deeper than anyone but Alex expected. Continuing with Alex's testimony regarding his initial meeting with the FBI, we learn:

> *Q. What was the date of that meeting?*
> *A. The date of that meeting was June 30, 2006.*
> *Q. What did you do during that meeting?*
> *A. During that meeting I started to outline some of what had happened with him and give him the story about CEP.*
> *Q. And when you say "him," who are you referring to?*

A. To Drew Grafton.
Q. When you said you began to outline a story on June 30th, 2006, did you outline the whole story?
A. No, I did not.
Q. Did you outline the true story?
A. No, I did not outline the true story.
Q. What do you mean by that?
A. There were portions of the story that I did not relay and there were portions of the story where I lied about the extent of the knowledge that Bryan Noel had.
Q. You lied to who?
A. I lied to Drew Grafton.
Q. Of the FBI?
A. Yes, I did.
Q. And you lied about Bryan Noel?
A. Yes, I did.
Q. In what way did you lie about Bryan Noel?
A. I lied by stating that he knew about the trading losses going back to 2003 and, also, that he had authorized the rates of return that would be produced on the client reports down to the specific percentage.
Q. And was that true?
A. That was not true.
Q. Well, why did you say it?
A. At that point Titan had taken so much money and Bryan had—Bryan knew of that loan, authorized that loan, and it became very easy to try to blame Titan for all the mess of everything that went on even though there were trading losses that happened going back to 2002 before Titan ever got involved. So as a result of that, I just blamed Bryan and lied about his knowledge of all that stuff going back to that time period.
Q. So aside from the Pinnacle loans, you tried to put the trading losses onto Mr. Noel.

A. Not that the trading losses happened but that he knew of the trading losses, which was not true.
Q. That wasn't true, right?
A. That is correct; that was not true.
Q. Prior to October of 2005, did Mr. Noel know about the trading losses?
A. He did not.
Q. What was the result of that meeting?
A. At that meeting I had worked out a plan whereby I was going to submit my resignation to Bryan Noel. But Drew Grafton stated not to do that, that they may need me for something related to some type of investigation that needed to be done.

Better You Than Me

At this point, we want to get out of the boat and put our feet in the water. In this manner, we can have a better sense of what Alex said. Once more, for clarity, we examine Alex's words:

> *and it became very easy to try to blame Titan for all the mess of everything that went on even though there were trading losses that happened going back to 2002 before Titan ever got involved. So as a result of that, I just blamed Bryan and lied about his knowledge of all that stuff going back to that time period.*

- "It **became very easy** to try and blame Titan for all the mess of everything that went on **even though** there were trading losses that happened going back to 2002 **before** Titan ever got involved." Noel became Alex's Jonah. "It became very easy" to throw Noel out of the boat in order to try to calm the turbulent waters that had grown to be too treacherous to navigate. It was wasn't just "easy"; it was "very easy."

- "So as a result of that, **I just blamed Bryan** and **lied** about his knowledge of that stuff going back to that time period."

As a result of Alex's apparent, though deceptive, full disclosure, admission and cooperation, he was presented with a deal: he was allowed to plead to one count of conspiracy to commit mail and wire fraud. Alex faced a maximum penalty of five years' imprisonment, a $250,000 fine, or both.

Noel was ultimately "indicted and arrested on one count alleging conspiracy to commit mail fraud, twenty-five separate counts alleging mail fraud, and two separate counts alleging making a false oath in connection with a bankruptcy proceeding." Alex would provide testimony in Noel's trial and, in the fullness of time, stand before a federal judge and be sentenced.

Noel was eventually convicted of twenty-three of the twenty-four federal charges. Those charges ranged from mail fraud and money laundering to conspiracy and bankruptcy fraud. The press release issued by the Western District of North Carolina on March 5, 2010, read as follows:

Bryan Noel Found Guilty by Federal Jury
Henderson County Man–Former Owner of CEP, Inc., Remains in Federal Custody Awaiting Sentencing

U.S. Attorney's Office March 05, 2010

Western District of North Carolina (704) 344-6222

ASHEVILLE, NC—*Former owner of Certified Estate Planners, Inc. ("CEP"), Bryan Noel, 40, of Hendersonville, was convicted today by a jury in U.S. District Court of criminal charges that include mail fraud, bank fraud, money laundering, money laundering conspiracy, making a false oath in connection with a bankruptcy proceeding, and making false statements to a bank. The criminal charges were filed in connection with Noel's investment scheme that resulted in losses of millions of dollars of innocent investors' monies. Noel's trial took place in U.S. District Court in Asheville, beginning on Wednesday, February 17, 2010 and continuing through Thursday, March 4, 2010, before The Honorable Richard L. Voorhees, U.S. District Judge. Today's announcement is made by U.S. Attorney Edward R. Ryan of the Western District of North Carolina.*

Joining Ryan in making today's announcement is Owen D. Harris, Special Agent in Charge of Federal Bureau of Investigation Operations in North Carolina.

The River Turns and Turns Once Again

The evidence at trial showed that Noel owned an estate planning firm in Hendersonville that targeted elderly retirees. Noel would hold seminars at local restaurants, offering a free lunch and pitching an investment program to the retirees that included a promise that their funds would be pooled and invested in the stock market. In fact, the evidence showed that, after collecting approximately $10 million for dozens of retirees, Noel diverted more than $4 million of the retirees' funds to his risky start-up companies, including a mineral exploration venture in Peru and a composite lumber company, both of which failed. Investors were not told of these diversions.

The evidence at trial further showed that, as the scheme began to falter, Noel sought and obtained a $1.25 million loan from Carolina First Bank in January 2006 by representing that the funds would be used to purchase equipment. In fact, Noel intended to, and did, invest those funds in the stock market to generate sufficient funds to replace the diverted retiree funds. Ultimately, however, more than $300,000 of these funds were lost in the stock market.

The evidence showed that in August 2006, Noel then applied for a home mortgage and home equity loan on his house totaling more than $1 million. To get these loans, Noel misrepresented his monthly income and falsely deny that he was a defendant in any lawsuits (when he was at that time a defendant in three suits).

Finally, when these schemes all collapsed, the evidence showed that Noel filed for bankruptcy and failed to disclose his $73,000 BMW on his bankruptcy petition, instead reporting a 10-year-old pickup truck with 131,000 miles on it.

Bryan Noel is presently in local federal custody where he has remained since June of 2009. Noel will remain in local federal custody until he is sentenced by Judge Voorhees. A date for the sentencing hearing has not yet been determined.

It is important to note that any sentence received upon conviction will be influenced by the Federal Sentencing Guidelines, which the Court consults in order to determine the defendant's actual sentence. Sentences are based upon a formula that takes into account the severity and characteristics of the offense and the defendant's criminal history, if any.

Following an investigation conducted by the FBI, Noel was indicted federally in June 2009 on 27 criminal counts. In October 2009 six additional criminal counts were added to the charges, which included money laundering conspiracy, bank fraud, making false statements to a bank, and money laundering. Noel is currently facing a maximum sentence of 20 years in prison on each of the conspiracy and mail fraud counts, alone. Each count further carries a maximum fine of $250,000.

The case was investigated by the FBI, and the prosecution was handled for the government by Assistant U.S. Attorneys Melissa Rikard and

An Endless Stream of Lies

Matthew Martens of the Charlotte U.S. Attorneys Office, Western District of North Carolina.

But as he testified, Alex's machinations did not stop at the point he went to the FBI. While "cooperating" with the FBI, he continued with his deception. In his words:

> *A. There were portions of the story that I did not relay and there were portions of the story where I lied about the extent of the knowledge that Bryan Noel had.*
> *Q. You lied to who?*
> *A. I lied to Drew Grafton.*
> *Q. Of the FBI?*
> *A. Yes, I did.*

There are two broad taxonomies of deception—concealment and falsification. The first form is relatively easy, because it is passive. The second form is much more difficult in that it is active. Alex utilized both forms in his dealings with the federal authorities: Concealment—"There were portions of the story I left out"—and falsification—"I lied about how much Bryan knew." Additionally, Alex referred to his narrative to the FBI as a "story." Alex told the FBI a story. It was a story comprised of concealment, falsification and some truth.

In Shakespeare's *Macbeth*, Banquo advises most appropriately with:

> *"And oftentimes, to win us to our harm,*
> *The instruments of darkness tell us truths,*
> *Win us with honest trifles, to betray's*
> *In deepest consequence"*

More to the point, the prime directive given to any newly appointed investigator is always "never trust an informant." Once again, someone had placed their trust in Alex, and once more that trust was proven to be

The River Turns and Turns Once Again

misplaced. As Assistant U.S. Attorney Martin acknowledged during Noel's trial, "It isn't a happy time when you learn your cooperating co-conspirator isn't cooperating." All cooperating co-conspirators tell the truth . . . until they don't.

At this point, deception was not a new tactic for Alex. He had concealed the trading losses from his partner for the previous four years and he deceptively sent out false quarterly statements. But why deceive now? Now that Alex had ensured "everything" was not going to fall on him, why would he deceive those in the position to help him the most? Once again, we must look to the self-interest principle.

Once Alex met with the agents of the FBI, his cooperation included wearing a hidden microphone while conversing with Noel and recording several of their subsequent phone conversations. His deceptive, manipulative tactics did not end with his initial meeting with the FBI, but rather flowed onward for years. Within the packaging of his agreement to cooperate, the determination to continue with his deception was concealed.

> *Q. Now, you testified earlier that you began making some recordings as part of your cooperation back in 2006. Is that correct?*
> *A. That is correct.*

> *Q. Mr. Klosek, what are you discussing with Mr. Noel at this point?*
> *A. What rate of return to show the clients for that quarter.*
> *Q. At this point, what had you been telling the government that—at this point, being in July of '06, what had you told the government about what Mr. Noel knew about the rate of return on the client reports?*
> *A. That he was directing those rates of return.*
> *Q. And was that true?*
> *A. That was not true.*
> *Q. And so what are you trying to do here with Mr. Noel?*

A. I'm trying to get him to state a rate of return, which is why he is perplexed.
Q. Because he hadn't done that before.
A. He had not done that before.
Q. Did the FBI know that at the time?
A. No, they did not know that at the time.

Don't lose the significance of what Alex has revealed in the above: He is making a recording of a conversation with Bryan for the FBI. Within this conversation, he is "trying to get him [Bryan] to state a rate of return" that he had never stated before. Within the conduct of one recorded conversation, Alex is endeavoring to manipulate Bryan into putting forth a rate to imply that he had previously set the rate. Additionally, he is striving to underpin his deception to the FBI, with regard to having told them that Bryan knew and had known for some time, that the financial statements were reporting false information. Literally, he was playing both ends **from** the middle. Is this what Shakespeare had in mind, when he wrote, "*In double knavery – How? Let's see*"?

Concurrently with his having gone to the FBI with his deceptive "story," as well as his self-serving machinations—all the while appearing to cooperate—Alex diverted and hid assets belonging to the clients of Certified Estate Planners. In his words:

Q. Was there a safe at CEP where cash was kept?
A. Yes, there was.
Q. And can you tell the jury about that.
A. There was a safe where cash was kept.
Q. During what time period?
A. During the 2005-2006 time frame, sometimes investors would bring in cash, not in the form of a check but actual cash, and Bryan stated that that really should not be deposited in the bank account for fear it might raise some kind of suspicion with the IRS. So there was

The River Turns and Turns Once Again

a safe that was placed in CEP's office that I had a key to and Bryan had a key to, and that is where the incoming cash would be placed.
Q. And who had access to the monies in that safe?
A. I did and Bryan Noel did.
Q. What happened to the money in that safe?
A. The money in that safe was used by both Bryan and me personally.
Q. Well, what did you do with the money you took from the safe?
A. In some cases that money would be taken and it would be used to try to get credit for some type of account gains. In other cases it would be stored at my parents' house.
Q. What do you mean stored at your parents' house?
A. There were times where some amounts of cash, maybe 2 to $3,000 at a time, were stored at my parents' house for safekeeping.
Q. When did you first tell the government that you were storing cash from CEP in your parents' house?
A. Sometime within the past two weeks.
Q. The past two weeks?
A. Yes.
Q. Had the government asked you repeatedly whether your parents had any involvement in this matter?
A. Yes, the government had.
Q. Had I specifically asked you that?
A. Yes, you did.
Q. What did you tell me?
A. I said no.
Q. Was that true?
A. That was not true.
Q. Did you ultimately tell the government that the money was at your parents' house?
A. Yes, I did.
Q. Then what happened?

A. Then that money was returned, the balance that was theirs, as well as some silver that was theirs as well.

Q. Anything else hidden at your parents' house in addition to the cash?

A. No.

Q. Any silverware?

A. Well, yes. As I stated, there was some silver there.

Q. What was used to purchase silverware?

A. Client funds were used to purchase that.

Q. Why were client funds used to purchase silverware?

A. During the time of 2005 and 2006, in an effort to try to diversify some of the funds, there were some purchases that were made of silver coins and silver flatware.

Q. Were there some silver bars as well?

A. There were silver bars as well.

Q. This was all stored at your parents' house?

A. Yes.

Q. Why?

A. At some future point I hoped that I could sell some of these things and maybe use some of that money to get back on my feet somehow. But that money did not belong to me.

Q. Had the government repeatedly asked you whether there was anything involving your parents concerning this matter?

A. Yes, the government had.

Q. And did you—and did you tell us that there was silver and cash and silverware at your parents' house?

A. Not until two weeks ago.

We don't want to lose this revelation within Alex's testimony:

- He kept client's money at his parent's house.
- Over the years that he had been *cooperating* with the government, he did not reveal the existence of these resources.
- When he was asked about any existing resources, he lied.

- He had also hidden silverware, silver coins and silver bars.
- At some future point he hoped to sell some of these things and maybe use some of that money to get back on his feet somehow.
- It was only two weeks prior to his testimony that he had revealed the existence of the hidden assets.

Are you wondering what had happened two weeks ago that brought about Alex's sudden fountain of honesty? Stay in the boat; we'll find out.

Alex, who had swept the financial legs and feet out from under so many people, had hoped to use what they had earned, to get back on **his** feet. Is this the mindset of someone who stood before the court and all who were present and declared, *"And it was never my intent to lose anyone's money or divert anyone's money or scheme anyone out of anything"*?

MISDIRECTION

Alex, in his deception of the representatives of the federal government, utilized a most subtle deceptive ploy—misdirection. While Alex had the government focused on Noel, he utilized that diversion to convert assets to himself. After all, it was just easier to blame everything on Bryan.

It was not enough for Alex that now everything was not going to fall on him. He wanted more. He wanted to do more. He wanted more and he did what he had to do to get it, as represented by his testimony regarding his plea agreement:

> Q. *Did you have a plea agreement with the government?*
> A. *Yes, I did.*
> Q. *Directing your attention to the summer of 2009, did you sign a plea agreement?*
> A. *Yes, I did.*
> Q. *I'm going to show you Government Exhibit 450. Do you recognize that document?*
> A. *Yes, I do.*
> Q. *What is it?*

A. *That is the plea agreement that was entered in June of 2009.*

Q. *Was that the plea agreement or is that the bill of information?*

A. *The bill of information.*

Q. *What does the bill of information charge you with?*

A. *Conspiracy to commit mail fraud.*

Q. *Now, this is the bill of information that was filed against you when?*

A. *This was filed in June of 2009.*

Q. *And did you agree to plead guilty to that bill of information?*

A. *Yes, I did.*

Q. *Let me show you Government Exhibit 45P. What is that?*

A. *That is the plea agreement for that bill of information.*

Q. *And did you sign that document?*

A. *Yes, I did.*

Q. *When was this plea agreement filed?*

A. *This plea agreement was filed June 12, 2009.*

Q. *And the plea agreement required you to plead guilty to that bill of information, correct?*

A. *Correct.*

Q. *And what was the maximum amount of jail time that you were looking at under that plea agreement?*

A. *Five years.*

Q. *Five years in prison?*

A. *Yes.*

Q. *Were you required to do anything under that plea agreement?*

A. *I was required to cooperate and provide truthful testimony.*

Q. *Looking at page 7 of the plea agreement, what does paragraph 24(a) require you to do?*

A. *"The defendant will provide truthful information about the subject charges and about any other criminal activity within the defendant's knowledge to any United States agent or agency that the United States designates."*

The River Turns and Turns Once Again

Q. As of the time you signed that plea agreement in the summer of 2009, had you been providing entirely truthful information to the government?
A. I had not been providing truthful information to the government at that point.

An article published in the *Henderson Times-News* on March 3, 2010, titled "CEP Fraud Case Takes a Twist," reported that during Noel's trial, Alex's father testified that Alex told him he was proud of what he did in assisting the FBI and seeing the search warrants executed. Proud? Of what could Alex have possibly been proud? How could Alex be proud, while knowing that his deceptions and diversions of assets were still in play? Can assisting in bringing a fraudster to justice serve as a source of pride, while, at the same time, one continues to be a fraudster? Could it be the pride came from the game of playing both ends **from** the middle?

As Alex testified succinctly, "I had worked out a plan."

Thoughts, Comments and Analysis

What are your impressions, to this point, with regard to this circumstance?

Exactly what do you know?

What is it that you **know** that you don't know?

What questions would you ask in order to know?

What steps would you take in order to know?

The River Turns and Turns Once Again

POINTS TO PONDER

Compare and contrast Alex's words from his sentencing below, to his testimony we have just read.

> *And it was never my intent to lose anyone's money or divert anyone's money or scheme anyone out of anything.*

01. Can Alex's statement above be reconciled with his continuing to keep assets that did not belong to him?

02. Can that same statement be reconciled with his continuing deception of the FBI?

03. Could it be that in Alex's world, the statement and his actions were not mutually exclusive?

04. Explain.

05. What questions would you pose to Alex at this point?

Content – Context Application

The owner–operator of a home building company pled guilty in federal mortgage fraud case. Eleven individuals had previously pled guilty for their involvement. Those eleven people included other builders, lawyers, a loan officer, a real estate agent, a paralegal and a notary public. In the case, involving expensive subdivisions, individuals would purchase the house from the builder at one price. The next step involved arranging for buyers for the property at a higher price. Finally, deception was involved in getting the mortgages to a higher level. The inflated prices ranged from $200,000 to $500,000.

01. With regard to the twelve individuals (who pled guilty) referenced in the above: how would a network of collaborating fraudsters develop?

02. If we were to frame the concept of fraud as a virus, how would it spread from one individual to another in order to form this network?

03. Could it be that others exposed to the metaphorical virus (the opportunity to participate in the scheme for personal gain) had a moral resistance to infection? If so, why are some susceptible and others resistant?

04. What questions would you pose to this individual?

CHAPTER SIX

HE LOOKED INTO A POOL
HE FELL IN LOVE
HE WASTED AWAY

NAVIGATION POINT AND HEADING → At this time, we want to back up just a bit and examine still another tributary and its subsequent flow into the larger stream of lies. The setting is February 2010. The location is federal court in Asheville, North Carolina. The trial for Alex's partner, Bryan Noel, is set to begin. Alex is slated to testify as to their criminal activities. Alex's **first deal** with the federal prosecutor has been taken off of the table because of their discovery of Alex's **continued deception** and **theft**.

AND THE DECEPTION BAND PLAYED ON

In his subsequent testimony, Alex articulated his continued machinations after his initial meeting with the FBI in addition to his providing similar, false information in his testimony in previous civil proceedings:

> Q. Mr. Klosek, I think when we left off at lunch we were talking about your original plea agreement and your cooperation under that agreement. Do you remember that?
> A. Yes, I do.
> Q. And I think you testified that you were not being truthful with the government under your terms of your plea agreement.
> A. That is correct.

Q. Let me show you Government Exhibit 35X, which is already in evidence. Do you remember that e-mail?
A. Yes, I do.
Q. I think you testified before lunch that you were sending this e-mail under the direction of the FBI; is that correct?
A. Yes.
Q. And the direction that the FBI was giving you at that time was based on what?
A. Based on the information I had provided.
Q. And had you provided accurate information at that point?
A. No, I had not.
Q. Did the FBI know that at that point?
A. No, they did not.
Q. Now, did there come a point at which your false statements to the government became known?
A. Yes, there was.
Q. And when was that?
A. That was February 4th of 2010.
Q. 2010. Two weeks ago?
A. Yes.
Q. And where was that, that that occurred?
A. That occurred at the U.S. Attorney's Office in Charlotte.
Q. And the U.S. Attorney's Office is what, where who works?
A. Where you work and where Ms. Rikard works.
Q. And why were you at the U.S. Attorney's Office on February 4th?
A. I was having a meeting with you both.
Q. For what purpose?
A. For purposes of trial preparation.
Q. And had you met with agents of the government since your December meeting?
A. I had not.

Q. So you told us in December that you had provided false information, correct?

A. Yes, I did provide false information.

Q. And you came back on February 4th.

A. Yes.

Q. So you came to Charlotte to meet; is that correct?

A. That is correct.

Q. And who was present at the meeting when you came on February 4th?

A. You were. And Mr. Jenkins and Ms. Rikard were present.

Q. And did that meeting begin with me asking you again whether Mr. Noel always knew about the trading losses?

A. Yes, you did ask that.

Q. And what did you tell me?

A. I said yes, that he had.

Q. And what happened after you told me that?

A. After that, information was provided going back to 2002 showing the extent of the trading losses.

Q. Let me be clear. You told me at that meeting on February 4th that Mr. Noel knew about the trading losses all along.

A. Correct.

Q. Was that truthful?

A. That was not truthful.

Q. And after you told us that information, what happened?

A. That information was provided about the losses on the trading accounts that had gone back to 2002.

Q. What happened in the meeting after you told us that false information?

A. I continued to lie.

Q. And did I continue to question you about it?

A. You continued to question me.

Q. And what ultimately happened?

A. I had not told Bryan Noel the extent of the trading losses.

Q. What happened in the meeting ultimately?

A. In the meeting? You asked me to leave the room at the point at which—

Q. And what caused me to ask you to leave the room?

A. When you found out I was lying.

Q. And how did I find that out?

A. That the results for 2002 had been generated.

Q. Did you ultimately acknowledge after I continued to question you that you were lying?

A. Ultimately, I did acknowledge that.

Q. And at that point you were asked to leave the room?

A. I was asked to leave the room.

Q. And go where?

A. Out into the lobby.

Q. For what purpose?

A. Until Rick Winiker could be contacted.

Q. Who is Mr. Winiker?

A. Mr. Winiker is my attorney.

Q. And did Mr. Winiker come to the office and meet with you?

A. Yes, he did.

Q. And after meeting with you, did you come back in and continue to meet with the government?

A. Yes, I did.

Q. And at that point, what were you informed?

A. I was informed that there would be a different plea agreement, that no substantial assistance would be offered, and I had the option to leave and cooperate no further.

Q. And what decision did you make at that time?

A. I made a decision to stay and cooperate.

Q. Why was your plea agreement no good at that point?

A. Because I had not adhered to the terms of that plea agreement.

Q. And specifically what term had you not adhered to?

A. The part about cooperating and providing truthful information.

Q. Did you, in fact, enter a new plea agreement with the government?

A. Yes, I did.

Q. Now, the first plea agreement exposed you to a maximum term of imprisonment of what?

A. Five years.

Q. Did you get a five-year limitation in your second plea agreement?

A. No, I did not.

Q. What was the limitation in your second plea agreement?

A. The second plea agreement is 20 years.

Q. I'm going to show you Government Exhibit 45Q and ask you if you recognize that.

A. Yes, I do.

Q. And what is that?

A. That is the bill of information for the new plea agreement.

Q. And what is the charge in that bill of information?

A. The charge is conspiracy to commit mail fraud.

Q. What's the date of that document?

A. The date is February 10th, 2010.

Q. Six days after your meeting? Your first meeting.

A. Yes.

Q. Let me show you Government Exhibit 45R. Do you recognize that document?

A. Yes, I do.

Q. What is it?

A. That is the new plea agreement.

Q. And did you sign it?

A. Yes, I did.

Q. And what day was it entered?

A. It was entered on February the 10th, 2010.

Q. According to this plea agreement, what charge are you agreeing to plead guilty to?
A. I am agreeing to plead guilty to conspiracy to commit mail fraud.
Q. And that's the Count One of the new bill of information?
A. Yes.
Q. And under this plea agreement, what is the maximum term of imprisonment to which you are exposed?
A. Twenty years.
Q. Four times the prior plea agreement?
A. Yes.
Q. Do you have any promises from the government that you're going to get any benefit from testifying today?
A. No promises whatsoever.

Q. Turning to page 6 of the plea agreement, does it require you to provide assistance to the government?
A. Yes, it does.
Q. And, specifically, what does paragraph 25(a) require you to do?
A. Provide truthful information.

Q. During the course of the last three and a half years, was the United States the only person or the only entity to which you provided untruthful information about your conduct?
A. Yes, it was.
Q. Were you ever deposed in any civil proceedings?
A. Yes. Yes. I was untruthful at those as well.
Q. And specifically, were you deposed by Frank Jackson?
A. Yes, I was.
Q. Who is Frank Jackson?
A. Frank Jackson is an attorney in Hendersonville.
Q. And who was Mr. Jackson representing?
A. He was representing some of the investors.

Q. And they had brought a lawsuit?
A. They had brought a lawsuit.
Q. And what's a deposition?
A. A deposition is giving sworn statements under oath.
Q. And did you give truthful statements in your deposition?
A. No, I did not.
Q. Did you repeat the same false information that you told the government?
A. Yes, I had

OUTFLANKED

In the testimony above, we find the reason for Alex's sudden *honesty course change*, occurring two weeks prior to this testimony that we addressed in the previous chapter. Alex did not state that he had experienced a realization that he should have been truthful all along. On the contrary, he was outflanked and maneuvered into a disclosure by representatives of the government.

Alex must disclose his and his partner's collective fraudulent activities. Additionally, Alex must face the accusations and credibility attacks of Noel's defense team with regard to his individual deception and asset diversions after having gone to the federal authorities with his fraudulent "mea culpa." How difficult it must be to appear convincing while having to admit, "I stole and I lied. Next, I lied and I stole, up to two weeks ago. But now I am telling the truth."

LABELING THE CASE

In his opening statement of the federal trial of Alex's partner, Bryan Noel, Assistant U.S. Attorney Matt Martin depicted the case as ". . . an endless stream of lies." His assessment was accurate on several levels: literally, deception was most assuredly rampant and on a figurative level his use of the term "stream" was most appropriate for the case. The investors' money certainly flowed away from them like water down a drain.

Alex Klosek did not look like a fraudster. At the time, he was a young man in his early thirties, pale skin, slight build, with a tendency to turn his head slightly to the side as he spoke. His occasional smile was pleasant enough. His voice seldom deviated from quiet and monotone. Alex was someone who taught evangelism classes and encouraged others to attend. With shoulders a bit rounded, he was not someone that would stand out in a crowd or quickly draw attention if he was in a room filled with people.

But to the over one hundred people from whom he helped to defraud from seven to ten million dollars, as well as to the federal government, who computed the financial harm at nearly fifty-five million dollars, he looked every bit the fraudster.

In reality, fraudsters come in all shapes, sizes, genders, ages and nationalities. In this case, the package deal for Alex was a highly intelligent, articulate graduate of Loyola College. An online college picture of Alex sitting at his desk looking up at the camera relates, "President Alex Klosek studiously tending to the work of the chapter . . ." In another picture, we find Alex relaxing with three young people. He has on a red, short-sleeved shirt with a white Styrofoam cup in his hand. He is laughing—a smile stretched across his face. Lastly, in an auditorium setting, we observe Alex seated and listening with others to someone who is "informing the students of career opportunities in accounting and finance."

But, once again, how did this transition happen? Based upon an external force, in this case heat, water can change from a solid to a liquid to a gas. We continue to wonder, how does a young man in such a short period of time go from "studiously tending to the work of the chapter" to methodically stealing and deceiving—diverting the accumulated resources of over a hundred lifetimes? Surely, it can't be what he decided upon while someone was "informing the students of career opportunities in accounting and finance."

Was there a fatal crossroad at which point Alex made a fraudulent turn? Perhaps the fraudster resided in Alex all along, patiently waiting for the precise set of circumstances to be released. Like a virus, patiently biding its time until something happens within the body—a trauma, a fever, a sudden stressor—allowing the virus to spring forth and take over.

Narcissus

In Greek mythology, Narcissus was a hunter. He was known for his exceptionally attractive appearance. He was just as exceptionally prideful and scornful of those who loved him. One day, he looked into a pool and fell in love with his own image. He did not realize it was simply a reflection. His love was so strong for his mirror image, he could not bear to leave, even just long enough to eat. He subsequently wasted away. This was divine retribution for his pride (Wikipedia). From this mythological illustration, we derive the concept of the "narcissistic personality." Narcissistic personality is defined as:

> *"Extremely selfish and self-centered, people with a narcissistic personality have a grandiose view of their uniqueness, achievements, and talents and an insatiable craving for admiration and approval from others. They are arrogant, exploitative to achieve their own goals and expect much more from others than they themselves are willing to give." (http://www.webref.org/psychology/n/narcissistic_personality.htm)*

A primary characteristic of a narcissistic personality is a strong sense of entitlement. This instance is not an entitlement, as in a legal sense of the meaning, but rather a self-imposed sense of entitlement. It is meant as a pejorative term.

At what point did Alex come to believe that he was entitled to that which belonged to others? Alex did not gaze into a pool of water and fall in love with his own reflection. Rather, he gazed into a large pool of money and fell into a sense of entitlement. He became enamored with what he **could take** and subsequently **did take**. Just as Narcissus could not tear himself away from the sight of his own reflection, Alex could not tear himself away from the sight of all that money.

As diverse as these two examples may seem at first, in the final analysis, each individual was focusing on what mattered most—himself. To Narcissus, no one was worthy enough to love him, or to receive love from him, but himself. To Alex, no one was worthy enough to have the assets that he took but himself. After all, he hoped to get himself "back on his feet at some point," with the resources of others that he had kept for himself.

We have learned, to this point, that for a number of years, Alex, while consistently losing money as a result of his stock trading—and well before he made his partner aware of the losses—was continuing to "withdraw large management fees" (34). At the same time, the partners were bringing forth company after company, layer upon layer, falsifying tax returns and selling additional people on the idea of trusting them with their money.

Another dynamic of the narcissistic personality is a lack of remorse—the inability to feel a negative emotion as a result of a wrongful action toward another.

Our analysis of Alex's voyage into the abyss can accommodate a variety of lenses—societal, the family unit, shifting mores, lost values and the combination thereof. But at the end of the day, the fraudulent voyage took place while other similar voyages are taking place at an increasing rate and, short of a cataclysmic event, will continue to do so.

Rather than quoting the data on the billions of dollars diverted by fraud each year, let's examine the efforts undertaken to keep us from becoming a victim of fraud. We purchase identity theft protection from companies, such as LifeLock, to enhance our security. Companies conduct background checks on prospective hires. There are mandated internal and external audits for publically held companies. A web search under "fraud protection" produces over 20,800,000 related sites. Cities, counties, state and federal law enforcement agencies employ hundreds of thousands of investigators and auditors in the fight against fraud. The private sector employs still more. The Certified Fraud Examiners Association—the premier fraud-fighting entity—has chapters throughout the world, all comprised of professionals united in the fight against fraud.

As I tell those participating in my fraud-related interviewing classes, "Whatever is wrong in society, is represented by some of those sitting across from you during your interviews."

Alex sat across from a great deal of different people—clients, a co-conspirator, representatives of the Federal Bureau of Investigation, as well as federal prosecutors. Through it all, time and time again, Alex manipulated things—reports, documents, funds—and he manipulated people . . . a lot of people. He deceived, when it would have seemingly been in his best interest to tell the truth.

Another example of Alex's manipulation of things came forth in his testimony at the trial. This element involved a home loan application. We read the following:

> *Q. Directing your attention to November of 2005, are you aware of a home loan application for refinancing that Mr. Noel applied for?*
> *A. Yes, I am.*
> *Q. Did you have any involvement in that?*
> *A. Yes, I did have some involvement with that.*
> *Q. Did you ever see the loan application itself?*
> *A. I did not see the loan application itself.*
> *Q. What was your involvement?*
> *A. My involvement was in preparing some documentation that Bryan said he needed to present to the mortgage company.*
> *Q. What kind of documentation was that?*
> *A. That type of documentation would include articles of organization and incorporation for CEP, and some type of letter stating that Bryan was the 100 percent owner, as well as something with a client account statement.*
> *Q. Let me show you Government Exhibit 45J, specifically the second page, and ask you if you recognize that.*

A. Yes, I do.

Q. What is that?

A. That is a client account statement for Bryan as of October 4th, 2005.

Q. And did you prepare it?

A. Yes, I did.

Q. At whose request?

A. At Bryan Noel's.

Q. Was it truthful?

A. As I recall, this is not a correct statement.

Q. And what was the purpose in preparing this?

A. The purpose was to show more assets in Pinnacle than what was really there at that point.

Q. For who to show more assets?

A. For Bryan to show more assets.

Q. Now, in the same time frame, November of 2005, did you have any discussions with Mr. Noel about Titan trading accounts?

A. Yes, we did, during that time.

Q. And when I say "Titan trading accounts," I mean distinct from the Pinnacle trading accounts.

A. Correct.

Q. Will you tell the jury about that?

A. Bryan was working on obtaining financing from Carolina First Bank which would be somewhere in the neighborhood of a million dollars, and his plan was to trade some of those funds via accounts that would be set up in Titan's name so that some of the gains that could be made off of those funds could be used to repay part of what Pinnacle's loan balance to Titan was.

Q. So you said in November of '05 that there was an application to what bank for a loan?

A. To Carolina First.

Q. And what—who was applying for that loan?

A. That would have been Titan Composites.

Q. And what was going to be done with those loan funds?
A. Those loan funds would eventually be used for purposes of equipment, operating expenses necessary for the business, but they would be traded in the interim.
Q. They would be traded. When you say "traded," what do you mean?
A. Traded in the stock market.
Q. And that was discussed when?
A. That was discussed as early as October, November of 2005.
Q. Did you take some steps to get ready for the receipt of those funds in the trading account?
A. Yes, I did.
Q. What steps did you take?
A. I opened brokerage accounts with two different brokers, AmeriTrade and Fidelity Investments.
Q. Was that your decision?
A. That was a decision that was made in conjunction with Bryan Noel.
Q. Let me show you Exhibit 45L and ask if you recognize it.
A. Yes, I do.
Q. What is that?
A. That is an account setup statement for Fidelity Investments. Well, for Titan Composites. I believe that's for Fidelity Investments.
Q. And who prepared that document?
A. That was prepared by me.
Q. Whose handwriting is on that?
A. That is my handwriting.
Q. Now, again, do you see up at the top right-hand corner what financial institution this is with?
A. That is with Fidelity.
Q. And in whose name, or what entity's name, is going to be on the account?
A. Titan Composites.

Q. Now, scrolling down to the second page, whose handwriting is on this page?

A. That is my handwriting.

Q. Is there a signature on there?

A. Yes, there is.

Q. What does the signature say?

A. It says Bryan Noel.

Q. Did Mr. Noel sign that?

A. He did not sign that document.

Q. Who signed that?

A. I signed that document.

Q. Did you have authorization to sign his name?

A. As far back as Digital Planet days there would be times when Bryan Noel would say that we could sign for him in certain instances, but on this instance I do not recall if there was specific authorization.

Q. Were you opening the account on your own initiative?

A. No, I was not.

Q. What do you mean?

A. This was done in conjunction with Bryan Noel.

Q. This Fidelity account in the name of Titan, were funds ever put in there to trade?

A. Yes, they were.

Q. Where did those funds come from?

A. Those funds came from loan proceeds from Carolina First.

Q. And were those funds traded in the stock market?

A. Yes, they were.

Q. Let me show you Government Exhibit 45M. Was the Fidelity account the only account opened for Carolina First loan funds to be received in?

A. No, it was not.

Q. Where else was an account opened?

A. AmeriTrade.

Q. Let me show you 45N and ask you if you recognize it.

A. Yes, I do.

Q. What is that?

A. That is the Titan account application for AmeriTrade.

Q. And whose handwriting is on that?

A. That is my handwriting.

Q. Now, do you see a name of an entity in the name of which this account is being opened?

A. Yes, I do.

Q. And what is that?

A. That is Titan Composites.

Q. And whose name is listed as the contact?

A. My name is listed as the contact.

Q. And on the second page, is there the name — is there a name there?

A. Yes, there is.

Q. And whose name is listed there?

A. That is my name.

Q. And does it list a title for you?

A. Yes, it does.

Q. What's the listed title?

A. Treasurer and president.

Q. Of what entity?

A. Of Titan Composites.

Q. Were you the treasurer or president of Titan?

A. I was not the president, and at that point I was not the treasurer either.

Q. Why did you write that down?

A. I thought this would facilitate the process of opening the accounts.

Q. Who was going to manage the funds in the AmeriTrade account?

A. That would be managed by me.

Q. And for whom were you going to manage the funds?

A. They would be managed for Titan Composites.
Q. Did funds actually go into the AmeriTrade account?
A. Yes, they did.
Q. And where did those funds come from?
A. They came from loan proceeds from Carolina First.
Q. Did you trade those funds?
A. Yes, I did.
Q. How did that go?
A. That did not go very well either. There were trading losses that were generated with those funds in 2006 as well.

A Societal Phenomena

Is Alex's manipulation of people and things nothing more than an aberration from the norm of society? More ominously, is Alex representative of the default setting on the societal ethical compass, displaying the go-ahead for:

- Situational ethics,
- Abdication of responsibility, and
- Moral ambiguity?

For example, many people purchase radar detectors to help them break the traffic laws and avoid the consequences of their violations. They mount the devices on their dashboards for their children to see and contemplate the unspoken message, "Do whatever, just don't get caught."

How narcissistic is it to believe, "I am entitled to break the traffic laws that are there for the safety of all"? How narcissistic is it to have no feelings of remorse regarding the dangers which speeding places on others traveling on the road?

Alex's device, capable of committing and hiding the fraud, was mounted in his head. The belief that he was entitled to do so was located in his heart.

Politicians lie to the public with reckless abandon. They lie about their military combat experience, as an example, and when discovered, they dismiss their falsification with, "I misspoke." Sadly enough, their electorate dismisses it right along with them by voting for their re-election. Perhaps, it is the collective mindset of "better the liar we know than the liar we don't know."

Professional athletes lie about or conceal their use of performance enhancing drugs. Statistically, one in four resumes or job applications contain falsifications or significant omissions.

Alex lied publically and privately. He was very much a part of *an endless stream of lies*. It may be that he was able to dismiss his own deceptive actions as readily as a politician or other notable deceivers. However, the public and the judiciary, in his case, were not so amenable to forget about it.

We will ascertain where the compass heading ultimately led in Alex's personal voyage. If we as a society are following that same heading, what will be our final destination? Only time will tell.

THOUGHTS, COMMENTS AND ANALYSIS

What are your impressions, to this point, with regard to this circumstance?

Exactly what do you know?

What is it that you **know** that you don't know?

What questions would you ask in order to know?

What steps would you take in order to know?

Points to Ponder

What follows is a portion of Alex's early testimony during the trial:

> Q. Mr. Klosek, when we left off, I think we were talking about the third and fourth quarter of 2002. You remember that?
> A. Yes, I do.
> Q. And we were talking about the client account statements that were sent out during that time period.
> A. Yes.
> Q. And I think you testified that during that time period you were lying to clients on their account statements.
> A. Yes, I was.
> Q. And you were lying to Mr. Noel about suffering trading gains — excuse me — experiencing trading gains when you were, in fact, experiencing losses; is that correct?
> A. Yes.
> Q. And I think you said that one of the reasons you lied was because you were fearful of losing your job.
> A. Yes.
> Q. At that point, is it fair to say that your work experience was one year at a CPA firm?
> A. Yes, it was.
> Q. And then one year at the company that went bankrupt.
> A. Yes.
> Q. And now one year at CEP, when you've been losing money for part of that year.
> A. Yes.

> *Q. Did you think you had particularly good employment prospects at that point?*
> *A. Not at that point.*
> *Q. At that point were you committing this scheme by yourself?*
> *A. Yes, I was.*

01. What were the motives, as presented in this brief testimony portion, for Alex to commit the scheme by himself?

02. If this were "one of the reasons" that Alex lied, what could have possibly been other reasons?

03. What perspective might a person have that is willing to lie to one hundred clients and one partner for his or her own self-interest?

04. What questions would you pose to Alex at this point?

Content – Context Application

A former public works director was charged with four counts of larceny by employee. The defendant was accused of keeping the money from the sale of discarded appliances. The appliances were part of the municipality's recycling program. The items were sold at a salvage yard as scrap metal. The proceeds from the sale were supposed to have been deposited into the appropriate governmental account.

When investigating a crime of this nature, consider the following:

01. How long did the individual work for the department of public works before becoming the director?

02. How long had the individual served as director before being discovered?

03. What ways might the individual have converted resources to himself, prior to becoming the director?

04. As director, what other ways might the individual have converted resources to himself?

05. What questions would you pose to this individual?

CHAPTER SEVEN

OIL AND WATER
DIFFERING TESTIMONIES

"Truth will rise above falsehood as oil above water."
—Miguel de Cervantes Saavedra (1547–1616), Spanish Novelist and Poet

Navigation Point and Heading → As a result of the efforts of Bryan Noel's defense team, the prosecution had learned of Alex's deception and continued withholding of CEP investors' assets. In open court, an incongruence between the testimonies of Alex and his father further served to muddy the waters.

Familial Conflicts

During the trial of Bryan Noel, a most telling drama arose—Alex and his father, Joseph Klosek, provided testimonies that were incompatible. Alex asserted as to what "did happen" and his father countered as to what "did not happen." Their two declarations were oil and water—they could not be mixed. And the reason they—oil and water, as well as the two Klosek testimonies—cannot be mixed, is an issue of "polarity." "Polarity" is defined as "the presence or manifestation of two opposite or contrasting principles or tendencies" (Dictionary.com). In the realm of linguistics, polarity is defined as "(words, phrases, or sentences) positive or negative character" (Dictionary.com). Both of their assertions could not be true.

In conditional logic, if Alex's testimony was true, then his father's words were false. Conversely, if his father's testimony was true, then Alex's words were false. Their statements were polar opposites—conflicting affirmations, sworn to in open court. And conflict is always at the heart of any chronicle.

Within literature, father–son conflict is a classic theme. For example, in Franz Kafka's, "The Metamorphosis," Gregor Samsa, a traveling salesman who was suddenly transformed into an insect, experienced such an ongoing dispute with his father. In Oedipus' case, the father–son conflict was most assuredly problematic for the whole family. Reading closely in Charles Dickens' *A Christmas Carol*, we find a brief and subtle intimation regarding a negative father–son relationship when Fan speaks to her brother—young Ebenezer Scrooge—in a dark, cold, wintery, deserted school house, saying,

> *"Father is so much kinder than he used to be, that home's like Heaven! He spoke so gently to me one dear night when I was going to bed, that I was not afraid to ask him once more if you might come home; and he said Yes, you should; and sent me in a coach to bring you. And you're to be a man!"* said the child, opening her eyes, *"and are never to come back here; but first, we're to be together all the Christmas long, and have the merriest time in all the world."*

But, for Alex and his father, evidence of a father–son conflict did not appear in the quiet and privacy of an empty school house. Rather, this conflict was made manifest in an open federal court with a court recorder taking down every word, the media reporting, the public most interested and the investors watching and waiting.

Was the pre-conversion Scrooge a product of a father that had not always been so "kind" and had not spoken so "gently"? Did the fact that home had not always been "heaven" produce a Scrooge that was, as Dickens wrote, ". . . a squeezing, wrenching, grasping, scraping, clutching, covetous old sinner"? If Fan had somehow lost her "fear" and had asked her father "once more," then we wonder, "Why and for how long had she been fearful, and how many times had she previously asked?" If now Scrooge's rank was to be a "man," had he previously been relegated by his father to that of a perpetual "child"? What role does the father–son relationship play in the making of the man? While Scrooge did not epitomize the "milk of human kindness" in his interactions with others, there was never an indication that he had ever stolen.

THE ASSERTION

In the trial of Bryan Noel, Alex testified that between 2006 (the year he went to the FBI) and 2009, he met with his father, Joseph Klosek, in order to obtain his help with the fabrication of the story he related to the FBI.

> *Q. After signing that plea agreement, in December of 2009, did you meet with the government again?*
> *A. Yes, I did.*
> *Q. Where did that meeting occur?*
> *A. That happened in Charlotte.*
> *Q. Where?*
> *A. In the FBI office.*
> *Q. Who was there?*
> *A. You, Mr. Jenkins, and Ms. Rikard were there.*
> *Q. And at that meeting, did I specifically ask you whether or not Mr. Noel knew about the trading losses from the beginning?*
> *A. Yes, you did.*
> *Q. And what did you tell me?*
> *A. I said that he did.*
> *Q. And was that true?*
> *A. That was not true.*
> *Q. Did you violate the plea agreement?*
> *A. Yes, I did.*
> *Q. In December of 2009, did the government know you violated your plea agreement?*

A. No, the government did not.

Q. In anticipation of that meeting in December of 2009, did you do anything?

A. Yes, I did.

Q. What did you do?

A. I had discussions with my dad about how to answer some of the questions that may be coming.

Q. Before your meeting with the government in December of 2009, you did what?

A. I met with my dad to discuss how to fashion some of the elements of the story.

Q. To lie?

A. To lie.

Q. You met with your dad to do this?

A. Yes, I did.

Q. Where did that meeting happen?

A. It happened at his house, as I recall.

Q. His house where?

A. His house in Horse Shoe, North Carolina.

Q. To lie about what?

A. To lie about the extent of the knowledge that Bryan Noel had as well as anything that may be potentially harmful to my dad.

Q. Well, what could be potentially harmful to your dad that you had to lie about?

A. The fact that we had discussed some of the story; the fact that he had access to Titan trading accounts; the fact that there were some things that were put into his home.

Q. So you mean you had met with your dad to discuss the story prior to December of 2009?

A. As I recall, there were some meetings prior to that time.

Q. When?

A. There were some meetings in 2006, but most of the meetings that happened were in late 2009 and early 2010.

Q. Mr. Klosek, are you telling this jury that you met with your father over the course of three years to provide false information about Mr. Noel to the government?

A. Yes, I am.

Q. Multiple meetings with your dad?

A. Multiple meetings with him.

Q. What in the world were you thinking?

At another point in the trial, the same topic emerged with the following exchange in Alex's testimony:

Q. Did you meet with anybody before coming to the U.S. Attorney's Office on February 4th?

A. Yes, I did.

Q. Who did you meet?

A. I had met with my father on the days before that meeting.

Q. For what purpose?

A. For purposes of trying to make sure that no information came out that was unfavorable to him.

Q. To lie?

A. To lie.

Q. To lie when?

A. To lie at any meetings I would have with the U.S. Attorney

THE OPPOSING ASSERTION

In a *Henderson Times-News* article on March 4, 2010, titled "CEP Fraud Case Takes a Twist," it was reported that, later in the trial, Alex's father, Mr. Joseph Klosek, was called to testify. In his testimony, he disclosed that he had been trading stocks since 1970 and had traded stocks for Certified Estate Planners. He testified that "he didn't know about all of his son's lies." He stated that it was not until after the FBI had searched Certified

Estate Planners, in late summer of 2006, that he became aware of his son's troubles. He further testified that he had never held any money for Alex, he did not meet with him in December of 2009 in order to fabricate a story, and he never purchased any property to hold for Alex. When he was asked if he had assisted his son in "fashioning a story for the FBI," he answered, "Never."

Alex had testified that they did meet and fabricate a story for the FBI (positive). Alex's father contented such a meeting did not take place (negative), inferring Alex was either mistaken in his testimony or deceptive—Polarity 101.

THE ISSUE REGARDING SELLING STOCKS

Let's focus our inquiry with the senior Klosek's revelation that he had traded stocks for Certified Estate Planners. How did he come to be in a position to do so? Did Alex approach his father, and if so, for what reason? There are a number of possibilities we can formulate for consideration:

In the first scenario, we can postulate that Alex went to his father with the idea of offering him the opportunity to buy and sell stocks with the investors' money in order to give his father something to do.

In our second theory, Alex's stock trading activities were going well, but he wanted them to do even better, so he brought in his father, with his decades of experience, to increase the gains even more.

The third case could be that Alex's stock selling endeavors were producing negative results, and Alex brought in his father to bail him out and get the project back on course.

In the last setting, Alex's father came to him and asked to be allowed to buy and sell stocks with the money investors had entrusted to Certified Estate Planners.

In his testimony, Alex provided an answer to our inquiry as to how the elder Klosek became involved:

Q. Did you seek any help with regard to the AmeriTrade account when you started sustaining trading losses?
A. Yes, I did.
Q. Whose help did you seek?
A. I went to seek the help of my father, who had traded stocks for much longer than I had, to see if there was something he could do with that account to maybe turn it around.
Q. Did he try?
A. He did.
Q. How did that work out?
A. I do not think that was successful. Initially it was, but with the ultimate result it was not successful.
Q. Were monies from the Carolina First loan that were traded lost?
A. Yes, they were.
Q. How much?
A. I don't know the exact figures, but I would approximate somewhere around $200,000.

So, we learn that it was Alex who initiated the process that resulted in his father trying his hand at trading stocks.

Regardless of the circumstance in which the senior Klosek began to trade, the relationship between father and son would seemingly, at a minimum, had to have been civil. In any case, Alex's father was, at that point, on board and performing Certified Estate Planners stock transactions for his son.

THE SOURCE OF ALEX'S STOCK TRADING ENDEAVORS

Back tracking a bit to regain perspective, we wonder, "How did Alex come to be responsible for trading stocks for Certified Estate Planners?" When Alex went to work for CEP in 2001, he had no stock trading experience. He had developed a stock trading program in college but had never tested the system. After the attacks of September 11, 2001, Alex "took over the management of Bryan's accounts because" he "told him about his 'stock trading system.'"

What do we know? The September 11 attacks produced an adverse effect on the stock market. Alex "told" Bryan about his untested stock trading system. "Told" means "to make known by speech or writing (a fact, news, information, etc.); communicate" (Dictionary.com). In one case, Bryan could have asked Alex, "Say, would you happen to have a stock trading program that you developed in college?" More likely, Alex may have initiated the idea when he "told" him about his system. In any case, Alex "took over" the "management of Bryan's accounts because . . ." "Because" is an explanatory term. An explanatory term is used to give the reason for or cause. It allows for the explanation of cause and effect.

The reason why Alex took over the management of Bryan's stock accounts was "because" he had told Bryan about his system. After Alex had made the information known, Bryan made the decision to turn the management of his own stock accounts over to Alex. Again referencing to the "best interest principle," Bryan now believed it was in his best interest to do so. This undertaking would be the first instance that "real money" would have been utilized in Alex's college-developed, stock trading system.

In his testimony, Alex reported, "In early 2002, Bryan was impressed with the results and thought it could be offered to clients of CEP." Apparently, the results of Alex's stock trading activities from late 2001 to early 2002 were positive as determined by the revelation that "Bryan was impressed" and "thought it could be offered to clients of CEP." Consequently, Alex testified, the clients of CEP were told "that their money would be invested into the stock market."

Alex testified that his stock trading continued to produce until June of 2002, at which point the investments started to result in losses. The investors were not informed that they were losing money. Alex prepared quarterly reports keeping the investors "up to date" with false information. During the trial, in an irony of ironies, Alex disclosed that he was sending falsified client reports to his partner, Bryan Noel, regarding the status of his personal investment, as he too was a client.

> Q. Well, we'll come to that. How was the trading going in 2003?
> A. It was not going well.
> Q. What do you mean?
> A. There were trading losses that were being generated above the trading gains.
> Q. So first quarter of 2003, were there net gains or net losses in the trading accounts for Pinnacle?
> A. I do not recall the exact figures, but most quarters during that time frame had more net losses than net gains.
> Q. During 2003, was Mr. Noel aware of the trading losses?
> A. No, he was not.
> Q. Why not?
> A. I had not made him aware of those losses.
> Q. Had you done more than simply not make him aware?
> A. Yes.
> Q. And what's that?
> A. I had continued to send out client reports showing rates of return that were positive.
> Q. And how were those client reports sent out throughout 2003?
> A. They were sent out via the Postal Service.
> Q. Now, during 2003, were you meeting with anybody with regard to your trading progress?
> A. Yes, I was.
> Q. Who would you meet with?
> A. I would meet with Bryan and—
> Q. How—I'm sorry. Go ahead.
> A. I would meet with Bryan and update him with trading progress.
> Q. How frequently were you meeting with him in 2003?
> A. On a weekly basis.

Q. And during these meetings, were you providing Mr. Noel with truthful information about how the trading was going?
A. I was not.
Q. What do you mean by that?
A. I was not telling him that there were trading losses being generated.
Q. Let me show you Government Exhibit 45B, which is not yet in evidence, and ask you if you recognize it.
A. Yes, I do.
Q. What is that?
A. This is a client account statement for Wild Kingdom Trust.
Q. And how do you recognize it?
A. This would have been among those prepared during that time, with figures that I used.
Q. You mentioned that this is for Wild Kingdom Trust?
A. Yes.
Q. And what's the date on this document?
A. The date is December 31st, 2002.
Q. So for what time period is this account statement?
A. This would have been the fourth quarter of 2002.
Q. And who is Wild Kingdom Investment Trust?
A. That was Bryan Noel's irrevocable trust.
Q. Well, why was he receiving a client account statement in late 2002?
A. Because he had invested funds into Pinnacle.
Q. And how much had he invested?
A. He had invested approximately 10 to 15,000 initially, and then there were subsequent additions to that during the course of 2002.
Q. So as of the end of 2002, what does this client report reflect was the opening balance on Mr. Noel's investment in Wild Kingdom Trust?
A. $46,729.61.
Q. Now, there's a column that says "performance"; is that correct?

A. *There is a column for that. And that performance figure is not correct.*

Q. *It's not correct?*

A. *No, it is not.*

Q. *What do you mean by that?*

A. *The interest earned would not have been that amount.*

Q. *Would it have been more or less?*

A. *It would have been less.*

Q. *Would it have been positive or negative?*

A. *It could very well have been negative at that point.*

Q. *Did you send this to Mr. Noel?*

A. *Yes.*

Q. *Why did you send this false account statement to Mr. Noel?*

A. *Because all clients that had funds invested in Pinnacle got account statements during the final quarter of 2002, and Bryan Noel did have money invested in Pinnacle.*

Q. *Well, why didn't you tell him the truth about how his account was doing?*

A. *I was terrified to tell him about what was really going on for fear of the consequences of losing my position.*

Q. *Let me show you Government Exhibit 45C. Do you recognize that document?*

A. *Yes, I do.*

Q. *What is it?*

A. *This is the account statement for Wild Kingdom Trust for March 31st, 2003.*

Q. *And how do you recognize it?*

A. *This would have been a statement that I had prepared with the figures that were being used at that time.*

Q. *What's the date on this report?*

A. *March 31st, 2003.*

Q. *What time period did this report cover?*

A. The first quarter of 2003.

Q. See the Performance column?

A. Yes, I do.

Q. Does it show that the performance has been positive or negative?

A. It shows it as being positive.

Q. Was that accurate?

A. That was not accurate.

Q. Did you continue to send out false account statements to Mr. Noel for 2003?

A. Yes, I did.

Q. And throughout 2003, did you continue to send false account statements to all of the Pinnacle clients?

A. Yes, I did.

Q. And throughout 2003 up through the end of November, were you doing this on your own?

A. Yes, I was.

Alex's relationship with his father is one tributary, and Alex's relationship with his partner is still another tributary. A commonality within the two relational tributaries is Alex.

Alex, in his relationship with his partner as shown by his testimony, was willing to manipulate things—the investor financial reports, for example. Additionally, Alex was willing to manipulate people—he concealed from Noel the continual investment losses. Additionally, he deceived the FBI with regard to the extent of Noel's knowledge.

Thoughts, Comments and Analysis

What are your impressions, to this point, with regard to this circumstance?

Exactly what do you know?

What is it that you **know** that you don't know?

What questions would you ask in order to know?

What steps would you take in order to know?

POINTS TO PONDER

01. If Alex was willing to manipulate all that he did in his relationship with his partner, to what extent might he do so in his relationship with others, to include:
    - Clients,
    - Federal prosecutors
    - Representatives from the Federal Bureau of Investigation
    - His father
    - Others?

02. What questions would you pose to Alex at this point?

Content – Context Application

An office manager and bookkeeper reached a plea deal with federal prosecutors regarding charges to include wire fraud and filing a false tax return. The bookkeeper reportedly took between $120,000 and $200,000 from the employer. The investigation was conducted by the Internal Revenue Service Criminal Investigation Division. The attorney for the bookkeeper described her as a "decent, lovely, wonderful person who cooperated completely with the government."

01. How do the descriptors *decent, lovely, wonderful* relate to the referenced fraud and the filing of a false tax return?

02. If the descriptors had been polar opposites—*decadent, ugly, awful*—would they have been factors to consider toward a different outcome?

03. What questions would you pose to this individual?

CHAPTER EIGHT

No Longer at Life's Helm
Into the City of Woes

There is a tide in the affairs of men
Which taken at the flood, leads on to fortune;
Omitted, all the voyage of their life
Is bound in shallows and in miseries.
　—William Shakespeare, *Julius Caesar*, Act IV, Scene III

Navigation Point and Heading → Now that Alex had pled guilty, the irony of ironies would spring forth: Alex—who in his undertakings to deceive, manipulate and control the resources and thus adversely distress the lives of so many people—would now find his own life in the hands of others. In that, Alex had abdicated control of his own destiny. Those within the federal office of probation would, through a complex maze of guidelines, evaluations, regulations, rationalizations and subsequent interpretations, place their hands on the ship's wheel of Alex's life.

All of these undertakings are designed for making a pre-sentencing recommendation to the judge, regarding Alex's punishment. For this voyage, others would set the sails, determine the destination and chart the course. Alex would become nothing more than cargo, to be off-loaded somewhere and for so long a time. This process would be the result of a ship's manifest, into which Alex would have no voice. In Alex's young life, the ship was going out with the rising tide and he was, for all practical purposes, tied to the mast.

What must it be like to know you no longer are the captain of your own fate? In Edgar Allen Poe's, "A Descent into the Maelström," there is an account of a man caught in an awesome whirlpool. His goal was to avoid being driven into the bottom of the whirlpool and perish. He desperately noted all that was going on around him. Like Alex, he formulated a plan. In his narrative he noted, ". . . that as a general rule, the larger the bodies were, the more rapid their descent." Additionally, he observed that ". . . a cylinder, swimming in a vortex, offered more resistance to its suction, and was drawn in with greater difficulty than an equally bulky body, of any form whatever." Continuing, he explained, "I no longer hesitated what to do. I resolved to lash myself securely to the water cask upon which I now held, to cut it loose from the counter, and to throw myself with it into the water." Alex had endeavored to lash himself to the strategy of his deception with regard to Bryan's knowledge regarding the false reports. After all, as he said, "It was easier." The plan devised by the character in Poe's story saved his life. Alex's plan had not been nearly so successful.

Alex, at this time, is most certainly caught in the whirlpool of the pre-sentencing, determination functioning of the federal courts. In the cargo-weighing operation of the United States courts, how large a body would Alex's machinations turn out to be? How rapid would be his descent?

The pre-sentencing, job-task responsibilities of the assigned probation officer are intricate in the extreme. A search of the United States Courts' website shows over fifty pages containing a list of various documents addressing the complexities. Additionally, at the website we find:

> *"The U.S. Probation and Pretrial Services System carries out probation and pretrial services functions in the U.S. district courts. Through its officers and other employees, the system works to make the criminal justice process effective and the public safe.*

> *The system's mission reflects its dedication to serve the community, the courts, and the people who come before the courts. The system's Charter for Excellence states the shared professional identity, goals, and values of probation and pretrial services officers".*

The probation officer's investigative protocol and subsequent finding are steered by an established set of ethical guidelines. The United States Probation and Pretrial Services' "Charter for Excellence" states the following:

> *"We are a unique profession.*
> **Our profession is distinguished by the unique combination of:**
> - *A multidimensional knowledge base in law and human behavior;*
> - *A mix of skills in investigation, communication, and analysis;*
> - *A capacity to provide services and interventions from pretrial release through post-conviction supervision;*
> - *A position of impartiality within the criminal justice system; and*
> - *A responsibility to positively impact the community and the lives of victims, defendants, and offenders."*

The Federal Sentencing Guidelines Manual contains the following:

> "***Authority***: *The United States Sentencing Commission ("Commission") is an independent agency in the judicial branch composed of seven voting and two non-voting,* <u>ex officio</u> *members. Its principal purpose is to establish sentencing policies and practices for the federal criminal justice system that will assure the ends of justice by promulgating detailed guidelines prescribing the appropriate sentences for offenders convicted of federal crimes.*
>
> ***The Statutory Mission***: *The Sentencing Reform Act of 1984 (Title II of the Comprehensive Crime Act of 1984) provides for the development of guidelines that will further the basic purposes of criminal punishment: deterrence, incapacitation, just punishment, and*

rehabilitation. *The Act delegates broad authority to the Commission to review and rationalize the federal sentencing process.*

The Act contains detailed instructions as to how this determination should be made, the most important of which directs the Commission to create categories of offense behavior and offender characteristics. The Commission is required to prescribe guideline ranges that specify an appropriate sentence for each class of convicted persons determined by coordinating the offense behavior categories with the offender characteristic categories".

The officer will begin a process to discover every facet of Alex's life. The officer will review the files of the U.S. attorney and the investigating agent's reports. Additionally, interviews with the federal agents involved in the CEP investigation will be conducted.

In Dante Alighieri's *Inferno*, Dante (the character) is guided by the Roman poet Virgil to a great river. The river is named Acheron and it marks the borders of hell. They are carried across the river in a boat. The boat is steered by an old man named Charon. At the top of the gates of hell, there is an inscription that reads, "THROUGH ME YOU ENTER INTO THE CITY OF WOES." Eventually, they come face to face with a monster named Minos. A long line of sinners stand before Minos. Eventually, each person stands alone before Minos and confesses their sins. Minos, then wraps his tail around himself a specific number of times. The number of times the tail is wrapped, is indicative of the circle of hell to which the sinner is assigned.

In the *Inferno*, there are nine circles of suffering depicted in hell. Each circle, from one to nine, represents a more reprehensible sin, with the punishment meted accordingly. There are no mitigating circumstances taken into consideration. The eighth circle of hell is for those having committed fraud. The eighth circle is guarded by a beast named Geryon. Representing dishonesty and fraud, Geryon has the head of an innocent man and the body of a serpent.

Alex's future now came down to the completion of a form by the assigned officer. This form is divided into four segments—A, B, C and D. The prefix to Alex's name would no longer be "Mister," but rather "Defendant." Whatever comprised that which was the essence of Alex as a sentient being would now be reduced to "Docket Number (Year-Sequence-Defendant No.)."

The first segment of the form is titled "Worksheet A – (Offense Level)." The initial instructions bear witness of the intricacies involved:

> *"For each count of conviction (or stipulated offense), complete a separate Worksheet A. Exception: Use only a single Worksheet A where the offense level for a group of closely related counts is based primarily on aggregate value or quantity (see §3D1.2(d)) or where a count of conspiracy, solicitation, or attempt is grouped with a substantive count that was the sole object of the conspiracy, solicitation, or attempt (see §3D1.2(a) and (b))."*

On this form there are blank spaces to be completed and boxes to be checked. Each blank and box is a determinate of Alex's future. A stream comprised of blank spaces and boxes carrying Alex to a destination that remains, at this point, too far around the turn to even be speculated.

The next segment is "Worksheet B – (Multiple Counts or Stipulation to Additional Offenses)." The instructions here require:

> ***Step 1:*** *Determine if any of the counts group. (Note: All, some, or none of the counts may group. Some of the counts may have already been grouped in the application under Worksheet A, specifically, (1) counts grouped under §3D1.2(d), or (2) a count charging conspiracy, solicitation, or attempt that is grouped with the substantive count of conviction (see §3D1.2(a)). Explain the reasons for grouping:*
>
> ***Step 2:*** *Using the box(es) provided below, for each group of closely related counts, enter the highest adjusted offense level from the various "A" Worksheets (Item 5) that comprise the group (see*

§3D1.3). (Note: A "group" may consist of a single count that has not grouped with any other count. In those instances, the offense level for the group will be the adjusted offense level for the single count.)

Step 3: *Enter the number of units to be assigned to each group (see §3D1.4) as follows:*

- *One unit (1) for the group of closely related counts with the highest offense level*
- *An additional unit (1) for each group that is equally serious or 1 to 4 levels less serious*
- *An additional half unit (1/2) for each group that is 5 to 8 levels less serious*
- *No increase in units for groups that are 9 or more levels less serious".*

The process increases in complexity, the formality begins to give way to subjectivity as the officer completing the form must now, "Explain the reasons for . . ." Now, no matter how professionally objective the person completing the form may be, opinions come into play—opinions with which others, including the federal judge that ultimately imposes the sentence upon Alex, may or may not agree. At this point, there are even more hands on the ship's wheel of Alex's life. More waters flow in and the stream begins to course just a bit faster.

In the third segment, "Worksheet C (Criminal History)," the officer delves deeply into Alex's past activities. The appropriate completion of this segment serves as a source of professional pride for the officer. No related detail of Alex's past is to be overlooked. The extreme detail for this portion involves, among other activities, obtaining letters of verification. The officer seeks to determine, "Who is Alex? What are his characteristics?"

The fourth segment, "Worksheet D (Guideline Worksheet)," is the longest portion, comprising four pages. The "Sentencing Options" portion is divided into zones A through D. Beside each zone is a box that can be checked. A check in a given box is a determinate for the course of Alex's life. Each zone provides criteria for the selection process. For example:

"Zone A If checked the following options are available (see 5B1.1):
  C   Fine(See 5E1.29a))
  C   "Straight" Probation
  C   Imprisonment"

Other segments in Worksheet D are: Length of Term of Probation, Conditions of Probation, Supervised Release, Conditions of Supervised Release, Restitution, Fines, Special Assessments and Additional Factors.

The Additional Factors section provides the most opportunity for the officer's narrative. The instructions for this segment are the most lengthy and involved:

"List any additional applicable guidelines, policy statements, and statutory provisions. Also, list any applicable aggravating and factors that may warrant a sentence at a particular point either within or outside the applicable guideline range. Attach additional sheets as necessary."

Would the fact that Alex had deceived the federal officials for four years and continued to divert assets to himself after having gone to them in 2006 serve as "applicable, aggravating factors" in the sentencing determination? At some point, because of his continued deception and actions, Alex's initial deal would be taken off of the table. No longer would the navigation buoy be set at "up to five years," but rather placed at "up to twenty years."

In the fullness of time, the form and the examination are completed. Copies are provided to the prosecution and the defense. They have two weeks to file objections. But there is just a bit more to consider—additionally, a "judge's eyes only" recommendation page is also prepared. On this page, the officer relays his/her "here's what I think" contribution. The complex and convoluted examination of Alex, his life and his actions all come down to one page. It is a one-page trip sheet playing no small role in the determination as to what would be Alex's next port-o-call.

Thoughts, Comments and Analysis

What are your impressions, to this point, with regard to this circumstance?

Exactly what do you know?

What is it that you know that you don't know?

What questions would you ask in order to know?

What steps would you take in order to know?

Points to Ponder

01. In your opinion, should mitigating factors be a consideration in Alex's sentencing determination?

02. If your answer to question number one is "yes," what are those mitigating factors and why should they be a consideration?

03. If the answer to question number one is "no," why not?

04. What questions would you pose to Alex at this point?

Content – Context Application

The U.S. Attorney's Office accused the vice president of a large banking enterprise of embezzling over eleven million dollars though a conspiracy scheme that operated over a nine year period. The fraudulent activities included false billing to the bank for millions of dollars' worth of home renovations, jet skis, golf carts, jewelry and other assets.

The accused worked as a vice president in utility services. Within that operation, his responsibilities included invoice payments. The invoices were submitted to the bank by contractors who performed worked for the bank. The contractors involved would return a portion of the money paid or provide other goods and services to the defendant. The contractors involved did not know one another, only the defendant.

01. Having reviewed the pre-sentencing determination, in the reading of this chapter, if you were the officer, how would you proceed?

02. In your mind, what could serve as mitigating factors in the sentencing determination?

03. If the vice president were a young woman as opposed to an old man, would that be a determination?

04. Would you eliminate mitigating factors altogether? Why or why not?

05. What questions would you pose to this individual?

CHAPTER NINE

Uncharted Waters

Why does the river rest so soon, and dry up,
And
Leave us to languish in the sand?
—Faust

Navigation Point and Heading → Alex has now come to a significant, transitional point in his voyage. It is the day and time for Alex to be sentenced. This is the point wherein the anchor of Alex's actions is to be weighed, and his ship of fate, set sail. There are a number of effecting dynamics that will function to set his course. The court, attorneys from both sides, a relative, Alex's wife, Alex himself, and victim representations will all have something to say at this ship's christening ceremony.

Change: Life's Only Constant

Each of us experiences the vicissitudes of life. This **is** life. Some changes are obviously positive, others painfully negative, while others are not easily determined until later on. But in most instances, life's transitions do not transpire in a public forum, such as a courtroom with reporters, spectators and others. Not so for Alex. Now, his manipulations of things and people will be hoisted like the flag of a pirate ship, for all to see.

The sentencing hearing will unfold like a Greek play. The play is titled *United States of America versus Alexander G. Klosek*. On the playbill, we will find the antagonist, protagonists, the aggrieved, the chorus and, implicitly, even Hermes. Hermes was the Greek god of transitions and boundaries. More importantly, he was the protector of thieves.

The transcript of the sentencing hearing reads like the actors' speaking parts. With the individual monologue, the character will walk onto the stage, speak their part and move to the side. In like manner of a Greek tragedy, it will all begin with the prologue, followed by the unfolding episodes. Throughout it all, only one person—Alex—will remain at center stage.

But this is not a play—this is life. Admittedly, perhaps, this sentencing hearing is life imitating art, but it is life nevertheless. Each actor will take their place on the stage and speak their lines. Some actors will be stage right and other actors will be stage left. The drama will continually build. There will be those who will advocate for Alex and others who will advocate against. Tension, like the strain on a ship's mooring line in a storm, will grow stronger.

There will be no dimming of the lights, but it will grow enthrallingly quiet. The play begins. We hear the sliding of the four feet under the chair as it is pushed back from the table. Someone stands, faces the court and begins to speak.

THE PROLOGUE: A GOVERNMENTAL REPRESENTATIVE ADDRESSES THE COURT

> *Your Honor, I won't add much. I'll say this. The decision regarding the filing of a 5K motion and then the extent of it in this case was certainly out of the ordinary and, I would suggest, fairly difficult for the government and persons involved in the case to wrestle with. There are certain facts, though, that I believe are quite compelling.*
>
> *First, when it started to come down, when the house of cards began to topple, we cannot ignore that it was Mr. Klosek that really took the first significant step of bringing it to the attention of federal law enforcement.*

I wish I could report to the Court at this time that that resulted in the saving of millions more dollars for purposes of restitution. Unfortunately, that was not the case. However, especially when comparing him to Mr. Noel—the Court even had the opportunity to hear this morning, he still lives in the state of he did nothing wrong—I must credit Mr. Klosek for coming—not only recognizing just how wrong it was, but recognizing the magnitude and bringing it to the attention of the FBI. That was important.

He then, in all fairness, almost undid everything, every bit of good he began, with his years of dancing around the truth—and that's not even a correct phrase—his utter ignoring of the truth for his part in it and also how it pertained to Mr. Noel. This was very significant because it was during this time that the government was preparing for trial, and Mr. Klosek, by necessity, was a very important witness for the government against Mr. Noel.

The prosecutors at the time, Ms. Rikard and Mr. Martens, both experienced and both very savvy, were relying an awful lot on what Mr. Klosek was saying, and literally right up to the eve of trial.

And Your Honor knows that very well. That had an awful lot of impact in terms of, number one, causing a continuance of the case and, number two, causing a great deal of disarray to the government's pretrial preparation.

At the end of the day, the foul did not result in enormous harm because Mr. Noel was properly convicted; however, Mr. Klosek's behavior during this time was significantly damaging.

And then he did testify at trial, and we believe he testified truthfully, we believe he testified effectively, and we believe his testimony has to be credited as substantial assistance for its part in leading to the conviction of Mr. Noel and, in fact, his sentencing today to 300 months.

So putting it all together, Judge, we ultimately had to fashion justice from it, and it is my submission to the Court at this time that we have done our best, and I believe we have made the right decision.

Episode One: The Court Speaks

The Court will grant the motion for a reduction for substantial assistance. The government has just described that assistance: that he went to the FBI in June of 2006 unprompted by any government agency; that that was the first indication the government had that a fraud was afoot; the government was able to salvage some of the victims' investments because of his assistance; and that to that extent it was timely and further enabled the government to build a stronger case against the co-defendant.

That is, of course, undermined to some extent by the fact that he was not totally truthful in the period leading up to the trial, but by the time of the trial, he had evidently come clean and told the truth and did testify.

The diversion of funds fraud was uniquely the scheme of Mr. Noel, albeit this defendant had knowledge of it, or came to have it.

Nevertheless, the stock-trading fund was the primary vehicle of the conspiracy; and in terms of the losses to victims, the diversion of funds was the greater producer of losses, and that was more directly assignable to Mr. Noel's involvement than Mr. Klosek's, who had little to do with the start-up companies and the diversion of funds to them, and virtually nothing to do with it apart from Mr. Noel's initiation.

Mr. Klosek's decisions were unfortunately influenced, that is, his decisions about cooperation, by undue influence from his father, who unfortunately was encouraging the defendant to lie and position his testimony in various ways.

That was, to say the least, unflattering as far as the father is concerned. Nevertheless, the Court mentions that in putting the defendant's cooperation and its shortcomings in context.

This defendant does pose a lesser risk of reoffending than Mr. Noel. He's more likely to seek legitimate employment after his release from prison. These are factors the government has cited in terms of evaluating the defendant's cooperation.

The government further points out that the defendant's assistance in the context I have cited was extensive and significant and useful. The government has assigned weight and asks for a 120-month sentence, and the Court gives that substantial weight in that the government's evaluation was not difficult to ascertain, nor is it difficult for the Court. But in the end, his testimony did appear to be complete and reliable.

And there were some risks of his cooperation in the sense that he wore a wire and was threatened by Mr. Noel in terms of the threat that he might become addicted because of some action on the part of Mr. Noel, or otherwise suffer consequences. So the Court evaluates that testimony and will make that a part of the sentence as we proceed.

Episode Two: Alex's Attorney Addresses the Court

Your Honor, in all candor, the Court's summary just now has taken the wind out of much of what I was going to say today, so that will even further reduce the time I will have before the Court. But I believe the Court has accurately assessed, as it has articulated already, the nature of Mr. Klosek's key involvement in this case. There are another few comments I'd like to add.

It's also not to be underestimated that it was because of Mr. Klosek going to the original FBI agent in this case that he was able to cause this to happen, that he was able to cause the best team, the

An Endless Stream of Lies

United States of America, to handle this—the scope of this kind of a case, to become involved to begin with.

I say that because I happen to have an entirely unrelated case, the clients were victims of a fraud scheme involving millions of dollars, that I've been trying to shop to different law enforcement entities for about a year. It ultimately may go somewhere. But Mr. Klosek was able to find the right agent at the right time and let him know what was going on, and by getting the FBI involved, that has brought us here today, and to bring Mr. Noel to justice, and to bring a million dollars in funds that had—you know, it has been said at different times there might be some sort of inevitable discovery of the fraud, but Mr. Klosek was able—because of the timing of this case, they were still able to seize almost a million dollars, which pales in comparison to the losses suffered by the victims, but certainly it's not an insignificant amount.

He wore a wire.

He was threatened.

He testified. He was part of the conspiracy, played a significant role, but performed at the highest level of cooperation that can be recognized by the government or the Court in every aspect of this scheme, beginning with voluntary self-disclosure all the way through testimony at trial.

The United States evaluated the harm, the relative harm, done by Mr. Klosek at the beginning of this case with the initial plea agreement, which was a 60-month cap. Mr. Klosek, not motivated by greed or willful ill-will or wanting to destroy the government's case or anything like that, but instead, I think, as observed by the Court, subject to the bizarre manipulation by his father, for no other explanation than a perverse desire to control Alex Klosek, Alex Klosek did not disclose the full extent of Noel's involvement in part of that scheme, but ultimately did and testified truthfully at trial.

And, obviously, as a trial attorney and as a former Assistant U.S. Attorney and as the attorney there on the ground with Mr. Klosek in the interviews initially with the United States, my heart goes out to the prosecution team of having to deal with this situation on the eve of trial. It's extraordinarily distressing and extremely regretful. However, Your Honor, with that in mind, the scope of what Mr. Klosek had done had already been evaluated, and the statements and the failures to disclose didn't change what he had already admitted to have done. He fully admitted to have been involved in the scheme. Now, he obviously made misstatements about when Noel was involved in part of one of those schemes, but Mr. Klosek had fully admitted to the scope of his wrongdoing.

And, Your Honor, it also bears mentioning that the scope of his wrongdoing, again, while perhaps motivated by greed in the sense that he was able to earn a salary during that period of time, he was not engaged in the siphoning off of millions of dollars for other investment vehicles and things like that. His wrongdoing was shame at having lost that money, and then Noel's, of course, siphoning off more funds until, for him, it came crashing down, and it was his guilt and his desire to do right at the end of the day that brought everyone here.

So it certainly is not—it's not laudable, and Mr. Klosek has—he will forever have this felony conviction as a mark, will forever have an enormously massive restitution judgment against him that will follow him the rest of his life. The rest of his life he will always be paying money back to these victims in this case. Every month. Every time he earns a cent, he will be paying money back for the rest of his life. He is penniless, his wife will need to move back home with her parents, and he's going to prison. He is—for all of his guilt, remorse, and the good works that he did when he recognized what was wrong, this man will be severely punished. This man would still be severely pushed even with the government's original assessment of the level of wrongdoing he had done, which is 60 months.

Now, I can understand entirely the government's recommendation of 120 months based on their experience in this case and the gut-wrenching situation that Mr. Klosek's regrettable actions put them in. However, I would argue to the Court that's not an evaluation of the 3553(a) factors in terms of the scope of what he has done in this case, the scope of what he has done to try to help rectify the wrongs, to bring a much worse man to justice, and considering the fact that he will forever be crippled by what he has done in this case, even with a prison term of 60 months in prison.

I can understand the government would want to double that, but, Your Honor, I would appeal to the Court as a dispassionate reviewer of this case and the ability of the Court to do the ultimate justice in this case.

Episode Three: Alex's Aunt Addresses the Court

Basically, I traveled here—it took me all last night to get here. And I'm ready to throw my notes away, to be honest with you, because a lot of the things that I was going to say have been said.

I can tell you that Alex is not the person—the person that I know is not the person who is being portrayed in the news media in Asheville when I looked for it online.

He lived with me during his college years, and during those years, instead of doing all the collegial things that he should have been doing I guess, he was doing budget plans for one of the poorest churches in the City of Baltimore.

He lost his brother, which affected him very, very deeply. His brother was his best friend. He also did all kinds of good things for people. When my mother had a heart attack, he helped me with her the whole time he was there.

Even last fall, he came up because he wanted to make sure that if he had to go to jail that he saw my mother again, and he changed doors for her, cut back shrubs for her, all the things—she's going to be 93 on her next birthday.

He told me about all this at one point when I was visiting him, and I said, "Oh, Alex, why didn't you just let somebody know," you know.

And he said, "Honestly, Aunt Pat, I thought I could get their money back for them."

And then he went on to tell me that he really liked the people so much and it was that much more hurtful to him because he liked his clients so much; they were such nice people.

So he felt a very, very deep sense of sorrow there. And as a result of doing the good things—as was said before, he initiated the contact with the FBI—he has lost his home, his vehicles, his credentials to practice his trade, which is being a CPA.

And he has never ever lived extravagantly.

He does not have big homes.

He doesn't take fancy vacations.

He doesn't have all the technological things that people like to play with. In fact, on the last family vacation, he and his wife, you know, slept on the floor in sleeping bags.

He's a very, very good husband to his wife. She is a cancer survivor.

He has been there with her through countless surgeries and all kinds of illnesses. And now he's facing the possibility that he's going to lose the simple pleasures of his life. I'm not saying that he's blameless, but he's a very, very good person.

In my daily prayers every single day, one of the lines that always strikes me is "Where there is despair, put hope," and it would be *my hope that you would give him hope and show mercy when you make the sentencing.*

Episode Four: Alex's Wife Addresses the Court

Thank you, Your Honor, for allowing me to speak today.

I'm sorry; I have a very low voice and I'm not feeling very well today.

Your Honor, I know Alex Klosek to be a loving, caring, dependable leader and a very loyal person. He is a hard-working, dedicated, God-fearing man who enjoys serving his faith and civic communities. I have personally witnessed him give a homeless man a shirt off his back and frequently lend a neighbor a hand when they need it. Further, though we have had—we've walked through much tragedy and strife in our first five and a half years of marriage, my husband has been a very supportive and faithful man to me.

Alex lived under long-standing control and manipulation by a very domineering father, which included having him take the blame—Alex—take the blame in covering up for his father's actions oftentimes. This was the source of what would otherwise have been seen as very bizarre behavior he had with the government last year. As I understand it, he was simply doing what he'd always done since childhood:

He had to cover for his dad's involvement in CEP, as his father demanded it.

He also had to cover for himself, because, again, he was following his father's orders.

I know this seems like very strange behavior for a man of Alex's age, but Alex had a very paralyzing fear of his father. Unfortunately, I believe Bryan Noel saw this vulnerability in my husband and used the same intimidation and manipulative dominance over Alex to get him to do what he wanted him to do, and I believe very strongly this was against my husband's better judgment. He was unable to stand up for himself or the clients as a result. Since his separation from his father and Bryan Noel, I have witnessed Alex become a much more positive and hopeful individual.

While I did not know the details initially, I observed Alex under an intense amount of stress related to his job at CEP. As time progressed, I saw that stress turn into complete anguish at what I grew to understand was the loss of client funds from his losses, Alex's losses, in the market and Bryan's scheming. Alex became increasingly depressed, even to the point of suicide, when he realized that the money was not coming back and he just couldn't fix it. I know he desperately wanted the clients to regain their money back and fix this situation.

His intent was never to harm anyone.

I firmly believe that.

Your Honor, I need Alex's loving physical, emotional, and financial support as I continue to battle with my ongoing health problems and a very uncertain future. His family also needs him to be able to provide them with a very positive role model that can change the trajectory for future generations from one of manipulation and unhealthy behavior towards responsible and godly life choices.

EPISODE FIVE: ALEX ADDRESSES THE COURT

I'm truly sorry for everything that has happened here, for the losses the clients have experienced, the life change, and everything that has happened. I know there have been serious negative repercussions. And it was never my intent to lose anyone's money or divert anyone's money or scheme anyone out of anything.

When I got out of college, I wanted to be successful and I wanted to be respectable, and when I started working at CEP in 2001 utilizing the trading system that I had developed in college, it seemed like that was becoming a reality, but ultimately, in 2002, things took a dramatic turn for the worse, and what seemed like it was a foolproof system started going bad late in that year, and I was very afraid to tell Bryan about that for fear of how he would react. And at the same time, in 2003, Bryan's new company Titan Composites was getting started. I know you're intimately aware of the details of all those transactions, Judge, and I won't go into great detail.

But I was approached to lend initially two and a half million dollars to Titan.

It was supposed to be on a temporary basis.

And I was not in favor of that initially, but when Bryan sets out — when Bryan Noel sets out to do something, he has a way of making sure that it happens.

And so ultimately that money was lent, more money was lent, and the cover-up got worse, the trading got worse, and basically, Judge, I feel like I got into a hole that I could not get myself out of. I was having to engage in riskier trades and doing things that were not helping to gain any of that money but, in actuality, ended up losing some more of those funds.

And I desperately wanted to get that money back, but after two and a half years without that money being returned, it was clear that there was nothing that I could do to fix the situation. It was not getting any better, and the only option I had was to get an attorney and to go to the authorities and tell them about what had happened with CEP.

Judge, words cannot express the remorse, the sorrow and the anguish I feel for these clients that are here today. I know that it has desperately changed their lives for the worse, and nothing would give me greater pleasure than to be able to repay every one of them everything that they had on paper that was invested within CEP.

I take full responsibility for my actions, Judge, for the wrong that I have done here and the consequences of those actions, and earthly success is no longer the guide that I use to measure things, as the way it once was.

Uncharted Waters

Episode Six: The First Victim Addresses Alex

First of all, Mr. Klosek, this sounds like you're a victim here. You're not. The victims are sitting right out there. Every one of us, we've been victimized. We're not your clients. We're your victims. Maybe you didn't intend it to be that way, but we are.

You did give testimony, I understand, against Bryan Noel, but it was the last minute, and it was to save yourself. It wasn't to help us. And as far as your marriage and your personal life, I think this is the second marriage, according to my first conversation with you. When you told me, "Mrs. Parker, your investments are safe, they are safe, you cannot lose this money," and the person that was sent to my house to take my money came five times and took the phone and got the money across the telephone, I think that's somewhat of a violation of using the telephone in someone else's house.

I got statements from your office which were bogus, and I think that is against the law, to send bogus mail through the mail. I think it's called a federal law to not send things through the mail that are fraudulent, which I got and I turned over to this Court.

And as far as you helping to come to a resolution with this, I think Roy Cooper with the state department probably did more for these victims than anybody, because we called him and we said, "What do we do," and he said, "You hire a lawyer," and we did — and we're still paying for it — or we wouldn't have gotten here yet. I still pay him. I pay BB&T every month for what you did, to pay for my lawyer. And BB&T bank told me: "Nobody, nobody, Ms. Parker, is paying this kind of dividends on your account. Something is wrong. We will check into it." And they did. The people in this courtroom are the victims Roy Cooper and the people sitting out there are the people that brought it to here. And as far as five years of your life being given up, I have spent the last ten years of my life trying to make up for the loss I have, and I still haven't made it up and probably never will.

An Endless Stream of Lies

I know your life is important, but so are all these old people sitting out here with these gray hairs, including myself. We're important. And as far as you being victimized by Bryan Noel, you're an adult. You are not taking responsibility for what you did. You're whining. I don't hear anybody out there except myself whining as much as I do you. You have not been victimized; we have.

And as far as you getting a lesser sentence for helping bring this to justice, huh-uh; you do not deserve that, and I do not recommend that. You're a young man, but you—still, you're a grown man, and you should have known right from wrong, and you should have not wronged all these people out of their life savings. As far as $2 million I hear, we're talking about $11 million, not 2. Where's the other money? I could have taken a heck of a good vacation on $11 million. Or even $2 million. I have worked the last ten years and I still haven't made up what you took. And I know that you are a computer genius, because you told me so. If you're a computer genius, you should have had better sense than to invest all those people's money in something you didn't know about. I think you broke a lot of laws, not one but many, and the most important one is the trust of the human beings that you dealt with.

And I know to be a fact I talked to you on the phone. I know that my money was wired from my house, my kitchen table, to your company, and I saw no dividends and never a dime back off from it. Not even a letter of apology. Not even a phone call. Nothing .Now, if there's so much remorse here, by George, I'd have written a thank you note for all that money you took and said, "Hey, I'm sorry I did this."

And I think it's a last effort on your part to sell Bryan Noel down the road. Which I'm not saying he doesn't need to go down the road; you both do. And that's all I have to say.

Episode Seven: A Second Victim Addresses Alex

I debated whether or not to speak at this particular hearing, sentencing hearing, but I listened to what Mr. Klosek said, and he said he didn't mean to hurt anybody.

In 2002, was it, you were aware that you were already losing money? In 2003 you were aware that funds were being diverted, and in 2004 you walked me to the bank to sign the papers to take my money away. If you didn't want to hurt anybody, that would have been a good time to say, "Ms. O'Ryan, this is not a good idea."

But you were protecting yourselves. More money in; it would not be found out quite so fast, would it? You falsified reports in order to keep customers and to protect yourself. We were honest. We asked for 1099s. We reported our gains to the federal government. I paid a thousand dollars in taxes because of gains that were fictitiously reported to me that the federal government has told me I cannot recoup because the time period has passed for me to file an amended return. I filed it, but they denied it. So that thousand dollars, you stole that, too.

You've imprisoned me in my home.

I can't afford to move to near my kids, and I have a grandchild on the way. The plan always was for me to move near my kids and help them when my grandchildren came. I can't afford to do that. I can't afford to change jobs. I couldn't help my son through a bad divorce and I couldn't help my daughter when she was refused and Mr. Noel stole that from me.

I respectfully request, Your Honor—this man has been walking the streets for the past five years, the same sidewalks that I walk. I don't want to see him outside again. I know he will get out. I know that we're asking for ten years; he's asking for five. Let me pass the next ten years without seeing him at a gas station and buying something. Please do that for us.

Episode Eight: The Third Victim Addresses the Court

Your Honor, thank you for letting me speak at this one, too. You heard what I went through the first time, which Alex has not. His wife talked about going through health issues. We've gone through colon surgery, colon cancer, chemo. Now we're going through lung. We've had gallbladder. So we've had a lot in the last four years, and this is because of stress that we've been through from losing all our savings.

And the thing about it is, I know Alex helped with Bryan, but he broke his plea bargain; he lied on the stand. He's been out for a year, walking the streets, getting to do what he wants to do.

What's all these people been doing? They've been suffering. He's just out living a free life. And I know that they're just asking for ten, but I agree with the other two ladies, and they said a lot more things that I would have liked to have said, but I think he needs more than ten years. Thank you.

Episode Nine: The Court Imposes Sentencing

Pursuant to the Sentencing Reform Act of 1984 and United States vs. Booker and 18 U.S. Code 3553(a), the defendant will be committed to custody for a term of 87 months. This sentence is sufficient but not greater than necessary to accomplish the purposes of 3553(a).

The Court recommends — the defendant has a history of mental health issues and recommends that he be allowed to participate in any available mental health treatment program while incarcerated.

Upon release, he'll be on supervised release for a term of 3 years. Within 72 hours of release from custody, he shall report in person to the probation office in the district to which he is released.

Uncharted Waters

While on supervised release, he shall not commit another federal, state, or local crime, and shall comply with the standard conditions adopted by this Court and the following additional conditions:

He shall be prohibited from engaging in any occupation, business, or profession requiring the handling of monetary instruments or securities unless approved by the probation officer in advance.

Further ordered that he pay the special assessment of $100.

The Court, having determined the amount of restitution, will order that it be paid as follows: The investors of CEP and Pinnacle, $10,513,465.67; Carolina First Bank, $91,572.02, for a total of $10,605—$10,605,037.69. That's the total. Any payment not in full will be divided proportionately among the victims named and listed in the presentence report and associated documents.

The defendant is jointly and severally liable for the total amount with Bryan Keith Noel, Docket No. 1:09cr57.

The gavel comes down, strikes wood, and that's it. If Hermes was indeed seen as the god of transitions and boundaries, this, for Alex, is most assuredly a transition. Continuing, Alex, who had, in the commission of fraud, broken legal as well as moral boundaries, now had a specific set of boundaries placed upon him—eighty-seven months of incarceration followed by three years of direct supervision and ten million dollar restitution.

Up to this point, we have been trekking upstream through various tributaries, seeking to understand the parts that made up the whole. With Alex's adjudication, we change our perspective one hundred eighty degrees. Now, we turn and look downstream. We turn from endeavoring to understand the past, to contemplating the future.

Where will the stream flow to from here? Traveling upstream is investigatory. Looking downstream is speculative. Immediately, we notice that there is a significant bend, just ahead in the stream. We can't see around it. What lies just around the bend? What water hazards, if any, are waiting patiently, biding their time, further on downstream? Or is it all just smooth sailing ahead?

There is a most telling scene in Shakespeare's *Richard the Second*. Richard, no small-time fraudster himself, is struggling with whether to abdicate and turn over his crown to his cousin, Bolingbroke. They meet. Richard speaks:

KING RICHARD II

Give me the crown. Here, cousin, seize the crown;
Here cousin:
On this side my hand, and on that side yours.
Now is this golden crown like a deep well
That owes two buckets, filling one another,
The emptier ever dancing in the air,
The other down, unseen and full of water:
That bucket down and full of tears am I,
Drinking my griefs, whilst you mount up on high.

HENRY BOLINGBROKE

Are you contented to resign the crown?

KING RICHARD II

Ay, no; no, ay; for I must nothing be;

It all comes down to water—in our continuation of water as a financial metaphor—in a bucket, doesn't it? That is the struggle, isn't it? Like the Apostle Paul pondered, "For that which I do I allow not: for what I would, that do I not; but what I hate, that do I" (Romans 7:15). Richard articulated well the vacillations of the inner chamber of the heart with, "Ay, no; no, ay"—yes, no; no, yes.

Barry Minkow became a convicted fraudster at a young age. Once out of prison, he portrayed himself as a "fraud fighter" and became a pastor of a church. Ultimately, he was convicted of embezzling three million dollars from The San Diego Community Bible Church—the face of an innocent man and the body of a serpent.

Paul: "But what I hate, that do I."

My grandmother, Lacy Watts Brown: "You can never tell about people."

Alex Klosek: "I had a plan."

Thoughts, Comments and Analysis

What are your impressions, to this point, with regard to this circumstance?

Exactly what do you know?

What is it that you **know** that you don't know?

What questions would you ask in order to know?

What steps would you take in order to know?

Points to Ponder

01. Do you think the comments of the victims played a part in the determination of Alex's sentence?

02. Do you think the comments of those who spoke on Alex's behalf played a part in the determination of Alex's sentence?

03. Do you think that the scope of Alex's sentence was commensurate with what he had done?

04. Why or why not?

05. What questions would you pose to Alex at this point?

CONTENT – CONTEXT APPLICATION

A city clerk with thirty-seven years of service was charged with embezzling over $45,000 of public funds. The embezzlement took place over a period of two years. In the warrant, it was stated that she diverted municipal funds directly into her own bank account. In her statement of admission to the law enforcement authorities, she stated that the stolen funds "did not go for vacations or such but did go to pay credit cards and help family members."

01. Should her stated reasons for stealing the funds be a factor in her sentencing?

02. Why or why not?

03. What questions would you pose to this individual?